We Are Still Here

We Are Still Here

Afghan Women on Courage, Freedom, and the Fight to Be Heard

EDITED BY

Nahid Shahalimi

PENGUIN

an imprint of Penguin Canada, a division of Penguin Random House Canada Limited

Canada · USA · UK · Ireland · Australia · New Zealand · India · South Africa · China

First published as *Wir sind noch da!: Mutige Frauen aus Afghanistan* by
    Elisabeth Sandmann Verlag, Germany in 2021
Published in 2022 in Penguin paperback by Penguin Canada
Simultaneously published in the United States by Plume, a division of
    Penguin Random House LLC, New York

Copyright © 2021 Elisabeth Sandmann Verlag GmbH
Pages 181 & 183 constitute an extension of this copyright page.

All rights reserved. Without limiting the rights under copyright reserved above,
no part of this publication may be reproduced, stored in or introduced into
a retrieval system, or transmitted in any form or by any means (electronic,
mechanical, photocopying, recording or otherwise), without the prior written
permission of both the copyright owner and the above publisher of this book.

www.penguinrandomhouse.ca

LIBRARY AND ARCHIVES CANADA CATALOGUING IN PUBLICATION

Title: We are still here : Afghan women on courage, freedom, and the fight
    to be heard / Nahid Shahalimi ; foreword by Margaret Atwood.
Other titles: We are still here (2022)
Names: Shahalimi, Nahid, 1973- editor. | Atwood, Margaret, 1939- writer of foreword.
Identifiers: Canadiana (print) 20220147078 | Canadiana (ebook) 20220147256 |
    ISBN 9780735246003 (softcover) | ISBN 9780735246010 (EPUB)
Subjects: LCSH: Women—Afghanistan—Biography. | LCSH: Women—Afghanistan—
    Social conditions. | LCSH: Women's rights—Afghanistan—History—21st century.
    | LCSH: Afghanistan—History—2001-2021. | LCSH: Afghanistan—History—2021-
    | LCSH: Afghanistan—Social conditions—21st century. | LCGFT: Biographies.
Classification: LCC HQ1735.6 .W4 2022 | DDC 305.409581/0905—dc23

Book design by Jennifer Griffiths
Cover image by Nahid Shahalimi

Printed in the United States of America

1st Printing

Penguin
Random House
PENGUIN CANADA

To my daughters, Ila and Mina:
I hope we leave even better paths for you
to walk on than the ones paved for us.

CONTENTS

FOREWORD

BY MARGARET ATWOOD

A LONG, LONG time ago now—in 1978, when people now forty years old had not yet been born—Graeme Gibson and I set out to travel around the world. Our destination was the Adelaide Festival in Australia, but you could get a round-the-world ticket that allowed you to stop along the way, so that is what we did. We had our eighteen-month-old daughter with us and felt that a single flight to Australia would be much too long on a plane for her.

The decision to stop in Afghanistan was mine. From the little I knew of history, I had been fascinated with it from afar. No foreign invader had ever succeeded in holding it long, including the British. Alexander the Great said, famously, that Afghanistan was very easy to march into but very difficult to march out of. The Russians were shortly to have the same experience, followed some decades later by the Americans. Why? Possibly the extremely challenging terrain, coupled with the ferociously independent spirit of the people.

Before we left, my father said, "Don't go. There's about to be a war." How did he know? Six weeks after our visit,

President Daoud Khan and almost his entire family were assassinated, ushering in the forty-plus years of warfare we have been witnessing ever since. We were lucky to have seen this spectacularly beautiful country just before it began to be torn apart.

Some say that Daoud Khan's encouragement of education and jobs for women was one of the reasons for his assassination. Whatever the truth may be, the position of women in Afghanistan made a deep impression on me—particularly their virtual invisibility in public spaces. Needless to say, this invisibility was one of the many influences—from both the past and the present, and from around the world—on my construction of women's roles in the Republic of Gilead in *The Handmaid's Tale*. I began writing that book in 1981, and it was first published in 1985, so you can see that my proposal of an American theocracy enforcing very limited roles for women came soon after my Afghanistan visit.

But what now—now that a puritanical theocratic regime has once more gained power in Afghanistan? Women who have been very active—as teachers, as scientists, as thinkers, as health workers, as creators—will be forced back into invisibility. They will be told they should not be allowed to have an education, because— here you may supply one or several of the answers that have been given, in many countries, in many times. Those answers have included women's incapacity for higher thought, their proper role as the bearers of children and the servants of the family, and so forth. Some in nineteenth-century Britain maintained that if women became educated, too much blood would flow to their brains, and their child-bearing organs would shrivel up. There has been no end of reasons, but none of them stands up to scrutiny. Let's say that one of the true reasons has to do with power and control, and the encouraging of a malignant side of human nature: the pleasure some take in inflicting pain on others.

Many women in Afghanistan have already disproven the idea that women cannot teach, learn, research, invent, cure, and create. Perhaps they will be forced into the shadows, hidden from view, their talents made unavailable to their country and their communities, but what they already know cannot be erased. I can't predict the future: I don't know how this amputation of women and their skills will affect Afghanistan. Perhaps younger women will be more despairing, as they did not live through the time when women moved from invisible to visible. Perhaps older women will be more tenacious, believing that what has been accomplished before can be accomplished again. In our strange and desperate times, plagued by a pandemic and by the brutal effects of the climate crisis, nothing is predictable. But as the Afghan women themselves have said, "We are still here." That in itself is a considerable statement: over forty years of turmoil and destruction, of rebuilding, of more destruction, they have been through so much.

A country without any women at all cannot exist for long. No matter how much a regime may hate and punish women, it can't do without them entirely. But what sort of women? We shall see.

INTRODUCTION
BY NAHID SHAHALIMI

FOR AS LONG as I can remember, we have not had time to mourn. One disaster has succeeded another. We have lost loved ones, our homeland, our freedoms, and our hopes. Now an entire nation and its youth are being denied what they require to even feed themselves and their families.

My Afghan friends and I do not have time to mourn because we want to help those who remain in our homeland and give voice to those who go unheard and may never be heard again. Radical repressive forces are now at work in Afghanistan, and this is of significant concern to all people of the world, but especially to women. Although Afghanistan is physically distant from Germany, which I call home today, radical ideas know no borders.

It is only by telling you about the past that you can truly comprehend what we once had and what we have repeatedly lost. And what we have lost once again with the Taliban takeover of Afghanistan on August 15, 2021.

My first trip back to Afghanistan in 2011, on Ariana Afghan Airlines, was twenty-six years after my family and I fled our beloved homeland. There were years when it

was not possible to travel to Afghanistan, especially from the 1980s to 2001, because it had become too dangerous. My mother, who had visited Afghanistan before 2011, and subsequently more often than I did, joined me on the trip. I was very excited. Over the past three decades, I had dreamed of what it would be like to return to my native land, but I could not imagine what my arrival would feel like in reality. To my surprise, there were many exiled Afghans on the plane—both men and women. Why were they going back to Afghanistan? Was this also their first flight back? These were questions I would have liked to ask the passengers. My fashionably dressed Western seatmate was twenty-five years old, born in Germany of Afghan parents, and had just completed her master's degree. Apparently, she wanted to see her fiancé, whom she had met at a large Afghan family gathering that is so common. It was her fifth trip to the country, and she had not a trace of fear.

I was overcome with a sense of belonging, and a feeling of happiness coursed through my entire body. I didn't realize how much I had longed for that feeling. For the first time, I understood what it meant to have a birthright. Among the other Afghans on the plane, I was not an outsider. We spoke one language, and I was on my way home at last. I not only wanted to see and visit the country of my birth after so many years, but I wanted to return to help: to get involved in building social and artistic projects, to advise, document, and report. Above all, I wanted to support women whose situations I could relate to and best empathize with. My destiny had always been clear; since I was twelve years old, I had longed to go back home.

I was lucky to live a few carefree years of my childhood in my country during times of peace and unity. When Mohammed Zahir Shah (1914–2007), the last king of Afghanistan, was overthrown in 1973, everything changed for my family. This overthrow ushered in the demise of our peaceful and united coexistence, at least as far as the forty years before the coup were concerned. The Soviet-backed communist government of the day was overthrown in 1978, and in December 1979, the Soviet army invaded Afghanistan, believing it could control the country. The Soviets became embroiled in a war with Afghan religious freedom fighters, also known as the mujahideen. The United States of America then stepped in, supporting the mujahideen with money and weapons. Afghanistan became the sad scene of a proxy war between the U.S. and the Soviet Union, with various other actors (such as Pakistan, Saudi Arabia, and Iran) also fighting for their interests and against the West. Over a million Afghans and about fifteen thousand Soviet soldiers died. When the Soviets left in 1989 after ten years, we did not have time to mourn the dead. A civil war followed between 1992 and 1996, in which another 1.5 million people lost their lives.

In the early 1990s, after the Soviet withdrawal from Afghanistan, the Taliban movement emerged in northern Pakistan; the word *taliban* means "students" in Pashto, one of the official languages of Afghanistan along with Dari. Upon assuming power, the Taliban pledged to restore peace and security in Pashtun areas along Pakistan's border with Afghanistan, as well as to enforce its own strict interpretation of Sharia, or Islamic law. It is thought that the movement originated from the harsh forms of the Sunni Islam religious Madrassas (religious schools) heavily funded by Saudi Arabia.

Because of the bloody civil war, the Taliban gained strength, and in 1995 and 1996 it introduced a radical and anti-human form of Islam promoted by Pakistan and Saudi Arabia. News that reached us in Europe then took on a new quality of terror.

Between 1996 and 2001, the Taliban terrorized Afghanistan and made no secret of its disregard for women. During that time, everything that could be considered joyful was banned: music, dance, sports. Women were only allowed to work in the health sector, and that was only because the mortality rate of women and children, especially in childbirth, had skyrocketed. Education for women was banned. Today, the rate of illiteracy among women in Afghanistan is still the highest in the world, especially in relation to the literacy rate of men. Education has proven to be an effective means of lifting both women and their families out of poverty, but that proved inconvenient to the Taliban.

The terrorist attacks of September 11, 2001, on the U.S. changed the world. Two passenger planes hijacked by bombers were flown directly into the Twin Towers of the World Trade Center in New York City, reducing the buildings to rubble. Two more hijacked planes set course for the nation's capital. One of those planes crashed into the Pentagon, and another crashed in an open field. Nearly three thousand people died. The terrorist network al-Qaeda and its Saudi Arabian leader, Osama bin Laden, who was hiding under Taliban protection in Afghanistan (and later killed in Abbottabad, Pakistan in 2011), claimed responsibility for the attacks. U.S. president George W. Bush declared a "War on Terror." Among other things, this war was intended to rid Afghanistan of al-Qaeda and Taliban networks. The fall of the Taliban in late 2001 brought us hope for a new beginning.

Although it was seldom reported by international media, Afghanistan changed as a new, young and dynamic generation came of age. In the years that followed, girls and women reclaimed many of their freedoms and rights. We truly believed there was a bright future ahead for them, free from the burdens of Taliban rule. In 2003, the new government even ratified the Convention on the Elimination of Discrimination Against Women, which obligated all thirty-four provinces to make gender equality part of their legal framework. It was not unusual for women to become ambassadors, ministers, governors, and members of the police and security forces. In 2009, a new law was introduced to prevent forced underage marriages and violence against women. At the same time, a promising democratic system began to take shape, and women from all corners of Afghanistan became increasingly active members of the country's social, political, and economic life.

As of August 15, 2021, there is little hope. The images on television and social media were like a slap in the face to me, and to everyone who feels connected to Afghanistan. The pain and shock were and are overwhelming.

The Taliban took control of the country under the watch of a stunned public. With control of the country, the Taliban took control of the fear of the people. Women did not dare to walk the streets, and those who aspired to education, participation, and personal freedom were safe only at home, as were those who worked for the allied forces and relied on the protection of those alliances. The images of the local forces attempting to reach Kabul airport in droves in August 2021 made headlines around the world. So did the news that men and women, old and young, could no longer leave the country. There were desperate attempts to reach neighbouring countries (Pakistan, Uzbekistan, Tajikistan, Iran), but most borders were initially closed. The Taliban's inability to feed more than 38 million people means that Afghans are prisoners in their own country and dependent on world hunger aid. In addition, there is a risk of renewed civil war, sparked by radical currents from the Islamic State (ISIL), which carries out attacks and aims to gain influence and power in the country.

While there have been nationwide protests by the population, even some initiated by women—and one of those women has her say in this book—the protests are life-threatening acts. The punishments for participating in them are draconian and the methods of punishment medieval. The Taliban, for instance, has been known to beat demonstrators and reporters with whips and cables. When I hear about these protests on Twitter, Instagram, and YouTube, and through other channels, I hold my breath, fearing the worst.

I remember very different years that seem like a distant utopia to me today. I was born in 1973 into a family where it was normal for a girl to attend school and university and later to take up a profession as a teacher, doctor, or scientist. Although the countryside has always been more conservative, in the cities men and women worked in the same offices and attended the same lectures. Those who did not want to wear a Chaderi, the blue full-body Afghan burka, or a veil were not forced to do so by law. In the streets of Kabul, the capital, young women wore short skirts. I have photographs of my mother and her friends presenting themselves in the latest Parisian fashions. Conservative Islamic values and liberal currents coexisted peacefully.

During my first eleven years of life, I enjoyed a privileged lifestyle. My family lived in a stately villa. My father, Abdul Hakim Shahalimi, had been a highly respected political figure before he retired from active political life in the late 1960s.

In 1981, my father passed away, and almost overnight our lives changed radically.

My father died because the communist government refused to let him leave the country for an operation that could only be performed abroad. They made that decision because he was not a communist. Not only were we in opposition to a political system, but the considerable fortune my father left to his wife and daughters became a threat to us. Women did not have the same rights as men even in those good times, and without a brother—that is, without a male representative—we were not worth much, except in men's fantasies that perhaps one day we would become attractive, docile wives. Some family members who were close to communism and who aspired to positions of power in the country, as well as others who claimed power and wealth for themselves, stole everything we owned. My mother was only twenty-six years old at the time, and when faced with threats of murder or the kidnapping of her four children, she decided to secretly flee to Pakistan with the support of my grandparents.

We couldn't take anything we once held dear with us. I understand the experience—or rather the trauma—of being displaced and having to leave everything behind: not just belongings but close family members and, above all, a place I called home.

In Pakistan, my mother worked hard to support us. In addition to being a talented seamstress, she had a natural talent for building things. She designed clothes for women in the neighbourhood and sewed Pakol hats, which were worn by the mujahideen and also popular with Afghans.

My mother, above all, wanted us to be educated. Education was also the most important thing among many of our Afghan acquaintances inside and outside the country. Despite this, homeschooling was the only option because we were the daughters of the renowned Abdul Hakim Shahalimi, who had led several ministries and became ambassador to several nations during the reign of the Shah of Afghanistan. In reality, we were political refugees and the heirs of the Shahalimi fortune left behind.

I hated our new life. In Pakistan, we had to wear huge veils that covered our entire bodies, and we hardly ever left our small apartment. We longed to leave, and we felt great relief when our immigration permits to Canada were finally approved.

When I stepped onto Canadian soil in my second home, Montreal, on a frosty December day—December 12, 1986, to be exact—my life as a refugee was finally over.

I immediately sensed that Canada would open up unimagined opportunities for me, and it did. Thanks to the incredible will of my mother, we were able to start a new, free life. Canada gave us a second chance. My sisters and I were accepted into an inclusion program that was among the best in the world. Our schooling was excellent, and we were all able to attend university.

During my studies, I played a lot of sports; my passion was volleyball. In my family, there have always been a lot of sports enthusiasts. Afghans love sports. One of my aunts was a very talented basketball and table tennis player and enjoyed martial arts; another was passionate about badminton. Some relatives, especially in Kabul and later in Montreal, had made begrudging remarks about the fact that women in our family played sports. However, it was my grandfather who encouraged his daughters and granddaughters to do so. He was one of many progressive men who found ways for their daughters and wives to be educated and to participate in sports, despite the conservative forces meant to prevent them. During my travels through Afghanistan as an adult, I saw many girls who were supported by their fathers or brothers to do something they otherwise would not have had access to. They flourished and beamed with happiness as they rode on bicycles or skateboards. Sports gave me strength, self-confidence, and freedom, and in war-torn Afghanistan, sports give women hope, self-confidence, self-worth, and body positivity.

Since first returning to my homeland in 2011, I have travelled there several times a year and met a great many women who courageously and fearlessly pursued their goals and who were true visionaries. In 2014, I decided to seek out inspiring Afghan women to interview them. I had heard many impressive stories that I wanted to share.

Over the course of nearly four years, I flew every two months to Kabul and to remote regions under sometimes challenging conditions. The women I interviewed ranged in age, social class, and ethnicity. Some had grown up in fundamentally different ways, some in the countryside, some in the city, and some in refugee camps. Such camps for internally displaced persons have existed for decades. According to the UNHCR, the UN refugee agency, "Afghans make up one of the largest refugee populations worldwide. There are 2.6 million registered Afghan refugees in the world, of whom 2.2 million are registered in Iran and Pakistan alone. Another 3.5 million people are internally displaced, having fled their homes searching for refuge within the country."

The women I met were proof that there was legitimate hope for a better future. With great perseverance, these women went their ways despite resistance and death threats—and in doing so, opened up new opportunities and paved paths for other women. They are great role models.

I met conductors Negin Khpalwak and Zarifa Adiba during one of my trips; they presided over Zohra, one of the first all-female orchestras in the world, when they were both under twenty years old. The orchestra has performed at some of the most prestigious venues across the globe, including the World Economic Forum in Davos, in 2017. It is now well known throughout the world. Adiba told me then, "We have a responsibility to rebuild this country. Afghans must not leave Afghanistan for a better future elsewhere." In the meantime, however, they too have left their country. When I spoke to them, they could not have imagined that there would again be a time without music, without instruments, and without singing.

The artist Shamsia Hassani, Afghanistan's first female graffiti artist, who taught in the Faculty of Fine Arts at Kabul University and who is now a successful artist world-wide, has also left the country. Art on public walls and façades as an expression of joy, free will, political courage, or even resistance will no longer exist.

I spoke with the young military pilot Shaima Noori, who confidently wore red lipstick, about women in the Afghan army. She described herself in the interview in a determined way, simply daring to be herself. Unfortunately, I was unable to find out how she is doing or where she is now, but I can say for certain she will no longer take off from an Afghan airfield as a pilot.

Today, I can watch only the past competitions of the impressive female Afghan athletes on YouTube. Some young athletes are still in the country and are in hiding, unable to practise their sport—be it soccer, basketball, volleyball, cycling, or skateboarding. I can only hope that they have found shelter and will survive.

I was also impressed by my meeting with Dr. Sharifa Yadgari, one of the very few psychotherapists in the country at that time who treated mental illness. In a country of severely traumatized people, including many women who are now more likely than ever to suffer from mental health issues, she was a beacon of hope. Now, whether she will be able to work in her field again remains uncertain. In 2017, she told me, "I also remember times as a child when I had no shoes, no school bag, and often not even pencils and notebooks. But I knew I had to make it, not only for my family and myself but also to be able to contribute to life in our community."

During my visits, there were moments when I survived only by a lucky accident. On December 11, 2014, I was invited to an event hosted by the Institut Français in Kabul. However, a day before that, I received confirmation for an interview with Maryam Durani, who had opened the first internet café for women and who ran Merman Radio in Kandahar, a Taliban stronghold in southern Afghanistan. I flew to Kandahar instead of going to the event in Kabul. Through this last-minute change of plan, I dodged a deadly suicide bombing at the Institut Français.

In 2017, my book *Where Courage Carries the Soul* was published. It was based on these journeys and conversations, and wherever I spoke about it, the event was sold out. The interest of the audience was huge, and interestingly, not only women came but also young men, including some with Afghan roots. They were glad to hear about women who had built something for themselves and their communities under such adverse conditions.

Yet the news about the 2018 negotiations between the Taliban and the U.S. in Doha, Qatar, should have startled us. Everyone—politicians, diplomats, negotiators—should have known that women would have nothing to look forward to, because not one woman sat at the negotiating table. The later invitation of a few was a purely symbolic act; no provision had been made to endow them with influence or power. What did the Taliban say in response to the questions posed during this round of negotiations about schooling, vocational training, and employment for girls and women? Did anyone ask them? As of today, girls will only be allowed to attend school until the age of twelve. Even then, the representatives of the U.S. and its NATO allies could have—indeed, should have—taken vulnerable people out of the country. Did they seriously believe that the Taliban would respect human and women's rights?

The new regime has removed women from the upper levels of the administration; women's voices are banned from the radio; women can no longer appear on TV; mirrors in offices and other buildings have disappeared or been painted over; barbershops and beauty salons have been closed; women can no longer travel long distances (over seventy-two kilometres) without a male family member accompanying them. The colours, the beauty, and the diversity are supposed to disappear, though Afghanistan is rich in colours. Our traditional clothes are colourful. We will not see them anymore. Even our flag has disappeared; instead, the colourless black-and-white flag of the Taliban flies. The Ministry of Women's Affairs was closed in September 2021 and replaced by the Ministries of Prayer and Guidance and the Promotion of Virtues and Prevention of Vice—morality police under the control of a Taliban minister. And, of course, the entire cabinet was made up of men. In the government of this "Islamic Emirate," no women were wanted or permitted. During an interview conducted in March 2022, one of the ministers even went so far as to say the only two acceptable places for a woman are at home or in a graveyard. The fact that some of the new rulers are among the world's most wanted terrorists is part of the irony of history.

In September 2021, *Time* magazine published its list of the one hundred most influential people of the year. Under the category of "Leader," it recognizes Mullah Abdul Ghani Baradar, one of the founders of the Taliban movement in 1994; he is described as "revered as a charismatic military leader and a deeply pious figure." As I read the write-up, my body flooded with the same excruciating fear and pain that I had felt in the weeks after the Taliban took power on August 15, 2021. At first, I thought it was a hoax. Someone must have hacked *Time*'s server. It just couldn't be, I thought to myself. Being included on the *Time* 100 list is an honour, a tribute; it is celebrated with a gala event in New York. It is inconceivable that the editors of the magazine could act in such a disrespectful way. They explicitly give these one hundred chosen people credit for changing the world, regardless of the consequences of their actions, and in so doing they insult Afghan women— and all women and girls around the world. Afghanistan continues to bleed. Self-expression is scarce. Journalists who criticize the new regime are subjected to whips and lashes. Is that considered impactful? Is that considered influential? Is that why this representative publication of the Western world, the so-called democratic world, chose to honour a Taliban leader as one of the hundred most influential individuals on Earth? Ultimately, his greatest accomplishment has been winning the war that defeated the most powerful countries in the world.

Over four decades of war and violence, as well as corruption and ethnically motivated hatred, have battered Afghanistan with extreme poverty and instability and traumatized its people. Nevertheless, the years that the U.S. and its allies were in the country—at least in the cities, which promised greater security, and sporadically in the countryside—gave an entire generation a sense of freedom and provided new opportunities for many girls and women.

The girls and women in my first book who embodied this awakening and a new vision of our country's future inspired all of us. But today anyone who is a visionary and proclaims her visions aloud puts herself in grave danger. As I write this, I wonder—as do all those who have their say in this book—whether we will hinder our own work and compromise our livelihoods with the words we say. There is still a need to censor ourselves for fear of being denied the support we all sometimes need for our work. Many Afghans who are committed to their country and to its women are forced—as I am—to remain politically correct in their language. Fundamentally, we do not adhere to the etiquette of the systems established for women—and this is true even in the so-called democratic countries of the world.

Working on *We Are Still Here* has been emotionally challenging. But when I spoke with these women, we shared and supported each other through the emotional, mental, psychological, and physical challenges we had encountered. For many, in the immediate aftermath of the Taliban's takeover, sleep was often out of the question. While there are those who managed to escape the country, many are still waiting to be rescued. You simply cannot imagine the fear when every day a shocking news story pulls the rug out from under your feet. Nevertheless, working on this book gave me the strength to believe in the future again. We have found strength in solidarity and in sharing with each other.

In the conversations that follow, women sometimes break taboos as if they have nothing to lose. We all agree that their achievements, made with great sacrifice and commitment, have not been in vain. We will not abandon the twelve-year-old girls who wish to continue their education, nor the female university students who had hoped to graduate, and certainly not the girls who are threatened by forced marriage.

No, we will not be silent and we will not remain in shock. We are still here! We must be heard. My appeal to you, dear readers of this book, is:

Listen to these women. See them. See their commitment to freedom and to their rights. See them in a new light. They are not victims. They never were.

They do not need regrets; they need a platform, support, and solidarity. Invite them to participate and bring them into your conversations. There are so many experts talking about us and our country. You can get first-hand knowledge from Afghan women. Afghanistan's women have proved time and time again how strong, resourceful, resilient, and forward-looking they are.

This time around, we will not be silent, for we are still here!

FERESHTEH FOROUGH

Fereshteh Forough is the founder and executive director of Code to Inspire, the first computer-coding school for girls in Afghanistan. She studied computer science at Herat University and completed a master's degree at the Technical University of Berlin. She is committed to gender equality and to the advancement and education of girls and women in tech. (This essay is adapted from interviews with Fereshteh Forough conducted by Nahid Shahalimi in September 2021.)

HAILING FROM HERAT, a city in western Afghanistan, my parents fled to Iran as refugees after the Soviet invasion. They had to start all over again, and I learned at a young age that entrepreneurship can start with nothing. My mother learned not only how to sew clothes but also how to sell them to earn money for our family and invest in her children's education. I am the fifth child of a total of eight siblings—five girls and three boys—and today we all have university degrees. If there's anything we learned from my parents' experience starting over in Iran, it's that what matters most is how you take advantage of the opportunities around you, regardless of where you are or what you have.

My father was a strong force behind us too. In Iran, he knocked on countless doors to secure the papers needed so that we could go to school. He's the one who encouraged me to pursue computer science, because, in his opinion, it was the field of the future. Unfortunately, it is quite rare in Afghanistan for families to support their daughters in pursuing their passions.

Though I was born in Iran in 1985, I moved to Afghanistan in 2002, a year after the fall of the Taliban and the U.S. invasion, to attend Herat University. I graduated with a bachelor's degree in computer science and went to Germany to do a master's program at the Technical University of Berlin. After that, I returned to Afghanistan to teach computer science at Herat University for about three years.

During my journey in education, there were many ups and downs, which led me to think about how to improve education for women in Afghanistan, specifically in tech. Most of the time, a female graduate with a degree in computer science wouldn't be able to find a job in her field. Code to Inspire (CTI) uses technology, education, and outreach to provide Afghan women with leverage in their fight for social, political, and economic equality. Well beyond simply providing education, CTI has become a grassroots movement that has shifted society's views on investing in girls' education, especially in the tech sector.

Our strategy since 2015, the year Code to Inspire was founded, has been to develop these areas. Not only have we educated women in the tech sector, we've also educated an entire generation of female leaders. These women have developed skills that open doors to employment. Between 60 and 70 percent of our female graduates have found work in their communities. In Afghanistan, our students have undertaken about forty projects, many commissioned from the U.S., worth a total of $35,000. Many of the women we've trained are now earning double or triple the wages of men.

General education and resources for women are crucial, but work in tech can facilitate even greater freedoms. There may be limited opportunities for work in Afghanistan, but with an internet connection, tech workers can work for clients all over the world. They can also work from the privacy of their own homes, which means future laws and restrictions won't curtail their work. Women will still be able to work, with a laptop and internet connection, no matter where they are.

The ability to make money also gives women greater influence at home and in a society like Afghanistan's, where it is primarily men who earn wages and make decisions. As soon as women bring money into their households, their voices begin to be heard. The fathers, brothers, and husbands of many of the girls we trained started to take an interest in what we were doing at our Code to Inspire school. Even though they don't understand what the girls are doing on their laptops, I think they like that they are earning money. In time, the men spread the news about our school far and wide, and many more family members and relatives started sending their daughters to learn new skills.

In my opinion, the generation that was born during the Soviet invasion—the so-called Freedom Generation—knows the value of education. Whether they were in exile or stayed in Afghanistan and lived under the Taliban regime in the 1990s, they have seen how those with college degrees have reaped the benefits of their education. In today's global economy, the educated can work from anywhere.

Our generation is also one that feels we should be free to expose lies without fear of being interrogated or having our freedoms restricted. This baked-in mindset will change the future of Afghanistan, no matter how long the Taliban stays in power or what laws it passes. It can't take that freedom away from us. Even if it cuts the internet, there are always clever ways to connect to the outside world.

Going forward, my top priority is to ensure that my students have jobs that bring them money and stability. But giving them face time with each other is important too. When they show up at school every day and see other women like them, they know they are not alone. Part of the work we do is to build a sense of sisterhood and solidarity among them. Now that they can no longer meet in person because of the Taliban takeover, their connections to one another are weaker. Still, the fact that female programmers can earn a living while safe at home is great for everyone. And it gives them the freedom to do whatever they want in a virtual world, no questions asked.

I'm a big fan of the Farsi poet Rumi. There's a Rumi quote I think of often that feels very apropos of what is happening in Afghanistan right now: "Where there is ruin, there is hope for a treasure." When one looks back at Afghanistan's history—decades of war, conflict, refugees, oppression—and compares it to today, as these events repeat themselves, all one sees is ruin. Ruined lives, oppression, and women locked away. But when one digs in ruins, there is always the possibility of finding something valuable. I see that possibility even in this very dark situation, where there seems to be no hope. I believe there are still treasures to be found.

To me, the girls of Afghanistan are treasures. If I can give them the tools they need to be the best they can be, Afghanistan still has a chance to grow. Both in technology and in peacebuilding, they are leaders. I still believe we will overcome our current challenges, and I'm trying my best to continue the work we're doing.

RAZIA BARAKZAI

Razia Barakzai was born in 1995 in Farah province, which is in the southwestern part of the country, near Iran. She studied political science at Herat University and has a master's degree from Kabul University. She worked as a university professor before being employed in various posts in the presidential office in Kabul. She initiated the first women's protests in Afghanistan after the fall of Kabul and is currently in an undisclosed location after receiving unequivocal death threats from the Taliban. The BBC named her one of its one hundred inspiring and influential women of 2021. (This essay is adapted from interviews with Razia Barakzai conducted by Nahid Shahalimi in September, October, and December of 2021.)

EVEN WHEN I was a student, I was always one of the strongly opinionated and outspoken girls—and whenever I spoke out, I did so in the name of justice. Like thousands of Afghan women, I grew up wanting to work, stand on my own two feet, and serve my homeland and my people.

Recently, my motivation to speak out has only increased. Though I was very young during the early years of Taliban rule in the 1990s, I have read books about them, heard reports, and listened to stories.

One incident stands out in my mind. Although it was a very early event in my life, I recall it vividly. I was out in the city with my parents—my father served as a commander for the security forces in Afghanistan and my mother was a housewife—and we were headed to the doctor that day. I was holding my dad's hand when a Talib on the street took notice that my mother wasn't wearing a Chaderi, the Afghan blue full-body burka. Having to watch that Talib beat my father ruthlessly for the offence is a painful memory I'll never forget.

Now, with the Taliban in power, once again women's rights are being abolished and the situation has grown urgent. I do not want to return to the despair of twenty years ago.

Toward the end of the 2010s, when I began working, I asked my parents to stay at home because of the growing instability in the country. Just like that, I became the breadwinner of the family. For a while I worked as a university professor in Kabul. At the same time, I also worked for the Independent Election Commission of Afghanistan for three and a half years. I worked in the president's office, which approved and implemented five of my projects, including proposals to build national peace parks in Herat and Nangarhar provinces and to create online feedback portals for complaints and petitions.

My last day at the president's office was Sunday, August 15, 2021. We were asked to leave the palace. I saw people in dire need running for their lives. The Taliban entered the presidential palace in Kabul that same day, and there was a sense of déjà vu in the air for those who had lived through the Taliban's first rise to power. Could this be an unwelcome repetition of what had happened over twenty years ago? It seemed that it was.

I turned my attention towards what could be done. I spoke with other young women from Farah province and we agreed that if we wanted to achieve our goals—which included defending our human rights and particularly women's rights to work, study, and move around—we had to stop being silent and speak out. To be silent would mean we were accepting and surrendering to the Taliban's power.

We decided to focus on two tasks. First, we wanted to protest, demonstrate, become the representative voices of Afghan women, and ensure our rights remained intact. We had not forgotten what had happened during the first phase of the Taliban's rule, when the deputy minister "for the promotion of virtues and prevention of vices," Talib Maulvi Qalamuddin, issued regulations that made women's lives a living hell. They included a ban on wearing shoes with high heels, because women are not supposed to make noise while walking; a ban on sitting in the front seat of a car; and a ban on male doctors examining a woman without a hijab, which meant women couldn't be examined by male doctors. We knew these rules would be reinstated and we knew we had to stop them. We also knew that being recognized internationally as a legitimate government was very important to the Taliban. If we were loud enough, we thought we might be able to counteract the disenfranchisement of women or even stop it completely. There was no way we could stay silent and allow things to backslide.

Second, we wanted to eradicate fear from the fabric of Afghan society by encouraging other women to join us in our protests. We wanted to show the Taliban that Afghan women were not afraid, that they were not the Afghan women of twenty years ago. Through social media, we reached out to a network of women, but many refused to stand with us at first. Some had deleted their profile pictures and replaced their names with fake ones out of fear. We tried to contact every single woman from all of the networks we had access to, but we received a negative response from almost all of them, except five. I was shaken by this turn of events. Why was everyone in hiding? I knew they were scared. We were also scared. But we were trying to channel our fear in a way that would preserve our freedom. Both because of and in spite of their responses, I remained convinced that we had to continue to act and fight. So, having managed to recruit five of them, we carried on.

On August 16, 2021, I set out with two women and decided to demonstrate in Zanbaq Square, at an intersection in front of the presidential palace in Kabul. We wore appropriate Islamic clothing to not appear radical in the eyes of the Taliban and some Afghans. This was partially because we were afraid of the reactions we would get from our friends and neighbours, in addition to the Taliban. The same daughters who are praised around the world for their courage are often disowned by their own families, and we were afraid of dying at the hands of our own people and becoming another Farkhunda. *Farkhunda* is shorthand for Farkhunda Malikzada, a twenty-seven-year-old student who, in March 2015, was beaten up and brutally murdered by a mob of angry men in Kabul, after being falsely accused of burning pages of the Koran in a mosque after arguing with a Mullah. Images of the event were circulated on social media and instilled fear in people across the country.

As we approached the presidential palace, we each held a paper leaflet that read, in Dari, Pashto, and English, "Afghan women exist." The guards noticed us and rushed over with their weapons. They tore up our papers without understanding what was written on them. They probably couldn't even read. (In man-on-the-street interviews with national and international media outlets and in social media posts, as well as in what we have observed at check-points, Taliban foot soldiers have repeatedly expressed their inability to read or write.)

We were scared, but I had spare leaflets in my pocket, so I distributed them. When an armoured vehicle approached us and someone inside asked what we wanted, we were shaking from head to toe. They told us to go home. I was more worried for my friends' lives than for my own, because I was the one who had planned the demonstration. I felt responsible. But everything was happening in public, and we were being filmed by cellphones from all sides, which may have saved us. The guards fear social media because the Taliban still seeks to appear tolerant and to give the international community the impression that it has changed since the 1990s—which, by the way, it has not.

Despite our efforts to dress modestly, the protests we led were opposed by many Afghan families. Two of the girls who had been on the road with us were not allowed to return home, because there were Taliban members living in their neighbourhood and their families felt that housing a protester would make everyone vulnerable. But there is also a general lack of support for women and girls across the whole of society. Afghanistan has always been a patri-archal and conservative society. It's nothing new.

After expressing our message in front of the presidential palace in Kabul, we moved to the Shahr-e Now neighbourhood, in the centre of the city. Our next step was to break the fear in society. Although many praised our courage and pride privately, no one raised their voice publicly for us out of fear. At our rallies, we endured insults from the Taliban and other men. "They want to make themselves important because they want to get on one of those planes," shouted one. "They are shameless," shouted another. But later that day, their voices were drowned out. Our hashtag, #AfghanWomenExist, started to spread on social media. It was incredible to see all the women who had originally refused to join us out of fear connecting with our movement. They no longer seemed to be afraid to post their photos online. And because videos of our protests had been posted as well, various journalists became aware of us.

Our protests had started very strong. In just a few days, the fear in society had broken, and there was an uproar across the country. We decided to take advantage of the moment and organize more protest groups with more women on WhatsApp. Within two or three hours, we had over three hundred members.

Unfortunately, the Taliban managed to infiltrate our groups very quickly, and some of our messages were forwarded as screenshots to Taliban intelligence. This meant that spies must have joined our groups. When I received a message addressed to me saying that we were infidels and apostates who should be punished under Sharia law,

I replied, "What crime, what sin have we committed?" In response, I received a screenshot of our WhatsApp group. The other activists in our group also received threats, and we had to move one of our members to an unknown location for protection.

As a group we decided to constantly change our location and spend our days and nights in different places. I received frequent text messages from the Taliban, sent from different numbers—sometimes even Pakistani numbers—threatening me with death. I learned from my friends that two weeks earlier two women, both teachers, had been killed in the town where I was born, because the Taliban thought one of them was me. The killers remain unknown, and shortly after the incident, news of my death was spread in the media.

After receiving a message addressed directly to me from the Taliban's deputy intelligence chief from Farah province, saying, "You will face harsh consequences," I decided to leave Afghanistan. I travelled secretly to Mashhad, Iran, hiding my identity papers on my body and wearing a burka for hours. But even there I was not free of Taliban spies. I have since moved again and live in another city.

Although we had gained support from various women's groups on the ground, our protests were sometimes met with violence: demonstrators were tortured and threatened with rifle butts, pepper spray, tear gas, electric shocks, and whips. As a result, we decided to carry out our actions at greater intervals, and we are working to strategically advance our movement through press conferences, articles, video clips, and online rallies. We even proclaimed October 10, 2021, to be World Women Solidarity Day with Afghan Women, and we saw global participation, both in person and on social media. Our groups are now much larger than the five women we started out with. Over six hundred activists from all over the world have come together in support of us, and our goal is to continue to grow that support. When Afghan women raise their voices, whether they are in Afghanistan or elsewhere, it is a sign of our unity and solidarity.

ARYANA SAYEED

Born in Kabul in 1985, Aryana Sayeed fled to Pakistan with her family when she was eight, made her way to Switzerland when she was twelve, and then went to London, where she studied business administration and began her singing career in both Afghan national languages, Farsi and Pashto. In 2011, she returned to Afghanistan, where she appeared as a judge on many popular TV shows, including *The Voice of Afghanistan* and *Afghan Star*.

During the years she spent in Afghanistan, Sayeed became an outspoken human rights activist. Following an unveiled appearance on *The Voice* in 2013, a group of clerics issued a fatwa against her on TV, promising entry into heaven to whoever could decapitate her. She was able to leave the country just after the Taliban took power in 2021.

FROM THE DURBAR (the palace of the Persian kings) to the homes of regular Afghans, music has been a vital part of the history and culture of my motherland for centuries.

The 1960s and 1970s are considered the golden age of Afghan music. Under the rule of the Afghanistan democratic government, artists had the freedom to pursue art and music. Radios and TVs were becoming fixtures in day-to-day life. Despite the conservative mindset of the average Afghan, music had always been part of family life for a good portion of the population. Especially in modern provinces and cities, you would rarely find a family without a singer, even if they just sang and pursued music as a hobby. At many private get-togethers, women sang for their own inner family circles. This slowly evolved and some began to pursue careers as singers. Many female entertainers have gained popularity in the years since, including during the last twenty years, although it still remained largely unacceptable for a woman to sing on television. Even singing on the radio was frowned upon for women.

While there has been much progress since the 1960s and 1970s, there have been periods when both music and female singers were scarce. After the Soviet Union withdrew from Afghanistan in 1989 and the Democratic Republic of Afghanistan under the leadership of Dr. Najibullah eventually fell, music and entertainment were sacrificed in the face of civil war. TVs and radios, along with all musical instruments, musicians, and singers, were silenced after the Taliban took over the country and banned music in 1996.

Now, at the time of writing, the Taliban has again begun to ban music in certain parts of the country, and many of us are wondering if the sounds of Afghan music will be scarce once again.

After the sudden and unexpected Taliban takeover of Kabul on August 15, 2021, the words *Kabul* and *Afghanistan* were featured on the world news more than any others. Kabul had become an indelible part of my life when I returned to Afghanistan in 2011, having fled the country with my family many years earlier as an eight-year-old child.

Our first stop on that journey out of Kabul in 1993 was the Afghanistan-Pakistan border, initially by vehicle, then on foot. Upon arriving in Islamabad, our first experience was with a not-so-friendly landlord, who was willing to rent his apartment only to a family of five, maximum. There were eight of us: my father (a tall and strong gentleman whom I remember suddenly aging ten to fifteen years, right before my eyes, during the first year of the civil war between mujahideen warlords), my sweet mother, five of my six sisters, and me. Thousands of people had fled Afghanistan and taken refuge in Pakistan, and there were so few apartments available. We had no choice but to lie about how many of us there were.

It was decided that my father, along with my mother and three sisters, would move into the apartment. Along with my two oldest sisters, I would stay outside until it was dark enough for us to sneak into our new home without being seen by the landlord or any neighbours who might snitch on us. While we successfully managed to sneak in that night, the landlord showed up the next day and we were revealed to be a family of eight. Sadly, we were kicked out; all of our belongings were thrown into the street and we were left in search of a place to sleep with a roof over our heads.

Eventually we settled in Pakistan, where I would spend the next four years of my life before I was sent— I should say, smuggled—to Zurich, Switzerland, at the age of twelve. I pretended to be the daughter of a Pakistani family and made the journey on my own to join my oldest sister and her daughters, who had been smuggled there a year earlier.

Fast-forward to the year 2000 in London, England. We had been taken there by yet another smuggler after our refugee case was rejected in Switzerland. By that time, I was a top student, and I spent a considerable amount of time in front of the mirror with a hairbrush in my hand, pretending it was a microphone, belting out tunes by Jennifer Lopez, Destiny's Child, and a few other top female artists in the Western world.

After getting my degree in business administration and working a few odd jobs, I decided to test my luck in the world of music and entertainment. I recorded some songs and a music video. It was 2009: the Taliban, which had come to power in 1996 and brutally ruled the country until 2001, had started to become a distant memory. And yet, with music being banned during their rule and life being very miserable for the people of Afghanistan during the civil war before that, there were not many Afghan women from younger generations who had pursued a career in music. As a result, I was approached to perform duets with well-known male singers of Afghanistan and received offers to perform joint concerts, even though I was still a rookie.

Around mid-2011, I received a call from Hasib Sayed, a Canadian-based concert organizer and founder of an entertainment and event management company. We had met on two previous occasions in Canada and Germany, and eventually he proposed to me and became my life partner. In 2011, Hasib was living in Afghanistan and had been approached by the country's biggest TV station, Tolo TV, which was interested in organizing a concert for me. Tolo made history by becoming one of the first private broadcasters in the country to offer a library of shows for viewers. It became an instant hit. Initially, I was quite hesitant. Afghanistan was not very safe; suicide bombings and terrorist attacks were slowly becoming a part of daily life. However, after discussions that lasted many days, and after convincing my family to approve of my visit to Kabul, I made the daring trip that would change my life forever.

While other concerts were recorded in the studios of TV stations, my performance was unique because I actually sang live on stage. Live musicians played by my side. Almost all of the concerts before mine had been pre-recorded as a playback. My concert was recorded live a few days before Eid al-Fitr, which is celebrated for three days and marks the end of Ramadan, the Muslim holy month of fasting. It was broadcast during prime time on the second day of the celebration. I became a household name in Afghanistan overnight and soon after became a judge on *The Voice of Afghanistan*, *Afghan Star*, and other programs.

I fell in love with Afghanistan after the concert, and for the next ten years, I spent half to three-quarters of each year in Kabul, appearing on various TV shows and performing concerts. But the concert also triggered a backlash from the Mullah's council (a council of Muslim priests). First, they took issue with the fact that I was not wearing a headscarf during my performance, and second, with the fact that I danced—just a bit, if I may be honest—during a couple of my songs. A warning letter was sent to Tolo TV. Thankfully, Tolo took it in stride. As the biggest TV station in the country, it was known to push boundaries and fight against conservative and extremist mindsets.

When I served as a judge on *The Voice of Afghanistan* during the month of Ramadan, one particular station, Noorin TV, brought a different Mullah on as a special guest every night for the first twelve days of the fasting month. Every night, they would speak exclusively about me for one full hour: about how I was a negative influence on society and the women of Afghanistan. On the thirteenth night, all twelve Mullahs came together and issued a joint fatwa, or decree, saying that anyone who cut off my head and brought it to them would go to heaven. At that point, we were in the middle of the season and I could not leave the show or the country. We recorded the show once a week, and each time I sat in my judge's chair, I feared someone from the audience might attack me and try to cut off my head. In Afghanistan, the promise of being sent to heaven is a powerful motivator. You may have heard, for example, that suicide bombers are promised seventy-two virgins in heaven after blowing themselves up.

For over forty years, the people of my country have dealt with an ongoing war, which grew out of a clash between those who long for progress and modernization and those extremely conservative-minded portions of the population that are stuck in the dark ages. The extremists believe women should stay at home, cook, and produce babies. For them, it is shameful for a woman to work a job outside of the home; pursuing a career as a singer is even worse.

While a very large portion of the population has always loved and supported me, there is another portion that simply despises me. It would not be an exaggeration to claim that I have heard or read the sentiment "You bring shame to our country and dishonour to the women of Afghanistan" over a thousand times in the ten years I served the country as an artist. Initially, I didn't even have the support of my own family. My manager at that time, and my fiancé today, Hasib Sayed, stood by my side like a rock and ignored the insults thrown his way.

Despite all of the opportunities I've had in Afghanistan over the years, I would definitely not have dared return without someone there I knew and trusted. And after my initial return, I would not have been able to take care of everything an artist has to deal with all by myself. The fact that I had Hasib by my side enabled me to stay in Afghanistan and pursue many other opportunities that have led me to where I am today.

Despite the constant threat of getting killed, my biggest fear when I was in Afghanistan was not death; it was being captured alive by the Taliban or one of the twenty-two terrorist groups NATO and the Afghan government had identified. My fear of being raped or paraded around in front of cameras kept me awake for many nights. Approximately eight years ago, I asked Hasib to promise that if I was ever in a position to be taken away alive, he would shoot me in the head. Of course, he would have to shoot himself in the head afterwards, or risk being held hostage himself.

That same promise was renewed when Hasib and I got stuck in Kabul after the sudden Taliban takeover in

August 2021. Completely in shock, we went into hiding at one of Hasib's cousins' houses. Even experts in the region were surprised. Nobody expected that an army of over 300,000 would simply dissolve and lay down their arms, despite possessing the latest American equipment and technology, in the face of a few thousand barefoot, ignorant, and vicious bearded men with turbans who were riding motorcycles. While the new Taliban regime made multiple claims about being more open-minded about the rights of women and the basic human rights of the Afghan people, its actions have proven otherwise. Given the uncertainty of the situation, we made a last-minute decision close to midnight on August 16 to leave and headed to the airport early in the morning on August 17.

Despite the many challenges I have faced over the years, unlike millions of my people who are still in Afghanistan, I have the luxury of a British passport. I can—and plan to—pursue my artistic career abroad. But my heart aches for the beautiful young women who looked up to me and wanted to stand on a stage themselves one day and raise their beautiful voices as Afghan singers. I am heartbroken to think of the even larger group of young girls who want to pursue their studies and someday serve their people as doctors or engineers or pilots. While I will continue to sing for my people and give voice to the voiceless, I am just not sure in the coming months and years how many of the beautiful women in my country—or even men—will be allowed to listen to my music or watch my music videos.

At the time of writing, the Taliban has prevented girls from attending school after grade six. They have forced almost all women who worked for the previous government—and those who worked for private companies—to stay home. They have begun to ban music in parts of the country. In so many ways, they seem to be the same dark-minded and vicious Taliban of 1996 to 2001. The only thing the international community can leverage is the funds promised to assist Afghanistan and its people during this very challenging period, and perhaps the fact that the Taliban is somehow hoping to obtain international legitimacy and recognition.

In the meantime, a new Afghan generation, often referred to as the Freedom Generation, is slowly coming to terms with the reality that they may not be able to pursue as normal a life as they did during the last twenty years. Girls and women who started feeling like normal human beings are being forced to become prisoners in their homes again. Men and women, young and old, are all living in a state of fear and trauma, with poverty and unemployment at an all-time high. Many of our people, including me, now believe only a miracle can save Afghanistan.

FATIMA GAILANI

Fatima Gailani comes from an influential aristocratic family and is one of the most distinguished women in Afghanistan. In Tehran and London, she studied Persian literature, Islamic studies, and Islamic law. She was part of the team that drafted the new constitution of the Islamic Republic of Afghanistan post-2001. She served as president of the Afghan Red Crescent Society (the Afghan affiliate of the International Federation of Red Cross and Red Crescent Societies) from 2005 to 2016. In 2020, she was one of four women who represented Afghanistan at peace negotiations in Doha, Qatar, with the goal of achieving an orderly transfer of power to the Taliban. (The following interview was conducted by Nahid Shahalimi in September 2021.)

When did you start negotiating for peace in Afghanistan?
I am one of the four women who participated in the Islamic Republic of Afghanistan 2020 peace negotiations in Doha. There I directly witnessed how hope for peace

has faded and how the country was taken over by the Taliban. But because I am convinced that the negotiations are not just a formal affair, I am still here in Doha trying to find a way forward. The negotiations that we have been conducting for over a year now—with a small break in January—need to continue.

I have also talked to the other three participants— Fawzia Koofi, Habiba Sarabi, and Sharifa Zurmati —who sat on the negotiating team with you, and I heard from them that there has been progress. Does this reflect your experience as well?

Well, if we had been realistic, there could have been progress and even an agreement. Most of us spent way too much time worrying about things that didn't exist. Watching the country collapse and eventually fall under Taliban control, that was very difficult. I have said all along that, in these situations, a formal agreement is better than no agreement at all, even if the agreement is not exactly what you really want or desire. But that is exactly what did not happen here. Not only did we insist on the constitution as a whole, but we also insisted that the Taliban join the republic, and you could see them waiting and just saying to themselves, *No, no, tomorrow we get the country back*. In those meetings, I said three times that we will rue this day of not finding a compromise. Because in the last

forty-three years I have seen that, without a political solution, we always lose.

In my opinion, anything that is formally settled, even
if it is not everyone's cup of tea, is better than nothing.
Today, we don't have an agreement. We can't complain
about what is happening in Afghanistan, because if there
had been an agreement with regard to women and with
regard to minorities, it would have been signed and sealed
today. Many of the values would not have been saved, but
maybe 40 or 50 percent would have been. Now we are
completely empty-handed.

Are there ways to build bridges with this new regime?
My experience spans over forty-three years. I witnessed
the communists take power. I was even declared crazy
when I predicted the Soviet Union's withdrawal from
Afghanistan. In the end, they fled the country. I believe
that negotiations and talks are still the right way today.
The people of Afghanistan cannot take another civil war.
It is rare that people die in armoured vehicles. But the
people who will continue to die are ordinary people who
have nothing to do with this war, who have nothing to do
with politics. Is that fair?

Which steps do you predict will be taken in the near future?

What has happened in Afghanistan is a reality. Although we have seen the shortcomings of the last twenty years with our own eyes, we have chosen to turn a blind eye to them. No one has demonstrated against it. We all say, "Oh, it was corruption, oh, it was nepotism, oh, it was this or that . . ." But did we demonstrate against it? Did we take to the streets? That was democracy, wasn't it? We could have done it. But we didn't! So what went wrong in Afghanistan? It happened step by step. Was there a point during the war when we as Afghans, especially we women, said to the government, "Enough is enough, the war must end now!"? Did we do that? No, we didn't.

Now that the foreign military has left the country, it is important that we—the Afghan people, who have always been good at blaming others—take matters into our own hands and begin a national discussion to solve the problem together. The women of Afghanistan don't want anything fancy. We don't want anything foreign, nothing that is foreign to Afghans or to Muslims. We women want at least a right that is common in the majority of Muslim countries. That is what we want: to open the doors that are now so closed.

The previous constitution, or let's say the last constitution of Afghanistan, which I was instrumental in, was
an Islamic constitution. Even then, there were people
who wanted to insert clauses into the constitution that
did not fit the Afghan culture. On the one hand, we had
to put the brakes on them, but on the other hand, we also
had to stop the radical forces. It was a good constitution,
but when a law is broken—for example, by corruption—a
crack is created, and when there is a crack, water spills as
from a broken vessel.

The new reality of Afghanistan today is the Taliban. We
have a choice. Planes can take away thousands of people,
but if the Taliban is to stay, we have to have talks. We need
to talk, and the Taliban should talk to the rest of Afghanistan. Otherwise, there will be a succession of wars. There
were mujahideen and various governments in the past,
and they brought the Taliban. They were needed to get
rid of the others. Then the same people who wanted to
get rid of them were brought in to fight the Taliban. Are
we going to continue this cycle? Is that justifiable?

**You are one of few who have been in direct contact
with the Taliban for so long. Now that they have nothing to lose, will they be willing to sit down with bridge
builders like you?**
Are you sure they have nothing to lose? They could lose
the country the same way the mujahideen did. Just like

the communist regime did. Just like Daoud Khan (the first president of the Democratic Republic of Afghanistan) did—because the crack started from him. So the crack will have to be repaired.

There will be no crack if all the people of Afghanistan consider this government to be an Afghan government, not a mujahideen government or a Taliban government or a communist government, but an Afghan government. In order to form an Afghan government, the Afghan people have to be involved. I envision a government where everyone has a real say. If the Taliban will not listen to the Afghan people, if they do not see reality, they will lose. But we also have to try to talk to them; otherwise, how will we know if they will listen or not if we haven't even started the conversation?

And how should the conversation start?
Well, we have to find a way—form a group, not just women, and then talk to them and say, "Look, we're not for anybody, we're for Afghanistan, we're for the people, and we want to end this war." What started in the Panjshir Valley [where resistance to the Taliban formed] could start in many other places.

How do you respond to those who want to leave the country? Who can help the girl in Afghanistan who wants to be an engineer but is not allowed to under the

**new regime and does not even have a passport to leave
the country? What advice would you give her?**

Not everyone in Afghanistan would leave the country
even if they could. I believe that we should not judge
people who have left their homeland. The diaspora of
any country can be very useful because many foreigners
who live in advanced countries like Germany, America,
or wherever, were and are supported there. Therefore,
I do not condemn those who left. Many may claim that
there were also many educated people among those who
left. I disagree with that, because there are many educated people who chose to stay in Afghanistan and could
not leave.

Those who wanted to leave recently and those who left
are a small minority. The majority are still in Afghanistan.
People who want to become engineers, pilots, surgeons,
or anything else according to Islamic values should be
allowed to do so. To do that, they have to pave the way.
We need female surgeons, engineers, and women in all
fields. So I think it is the duty of the government to pave
the way for the education of these girls.

Is there a message you would like to send to the world?

I am tired of telling the world what to do, because one day
it will leave you alone again after all. Our people should
know this: our country needs to be repaired, *we* need to

come together, and no matter what happens, *we* need to do everything we can to prevent another war. There is hunger in Afghanistan, people have not been paid, and the drought is making life very difficult.

And if I were really talking to the international community, I would say that for now we should separate the humanitarian and political efforts.

WASLAT
HASRAT-NAZIMI

Waslat Hasrat-Nazimi fled Afghanistan with her family in 1992 to Germany, where she currently lives. A graduate of political science and media studies, she works as a journalist and presenter for Deutsche Welle in Germany, a state-owned international broadcaster, leading its Afghanistan editorial departments in Dari and Pashto.

MY STORY BEGINS in Afghanistan, where I was born as the first of four children in Kabul in 1988.

While my mother worked as a news anchor for Afghan state television, my father studied medicine and took care of me on the side. A man looking after his child while his wife went to work was a rarity then, as it is now. Both men and women made fun of him and questioned his masculinity, but the teasing did not stop my father from caring for me and my sister. When he attended lectures, he would take me to the kindergarten attached to the university.

Despite growing up in an ultra-patriarchal society like Afghanistan's (or perhaps because of it), my mother had a self-confidence that is usually reserved for men in Afghanistan. She was a journalist and news anchor, which meant she was often at work in the evenings. Together with my father, my sister and I would sit in our apartment in Macroyan, a left-leaning and modern district of Kabul, and watch the evening news, starring my mother, one of the first female news anchors in the country. Seeing her on television was not only normal for us, it was also strengthening and encouraging.

It's clear to me that any confidence I have today was passed down to me from my parents—especially my mother. In the months before the mujahideen took over the country, the management at the television network asked all of the women who appeared on camera, including my mother, to cover themselves with a headscarf. This was meant to appease the mujahideen fighters. Once the mujahideen were in power, management hoped their behaviour towards the network would be mild and perhaps the network wouldn't get shut down. In response to this political exercise, my mother led a strike that continued until the network allowed her and the other women to anchor without a hijab. She believed every woman should wear what they wanted, and she didn't back down until she and her colleagues were given that freedom. My hope for every young woman in Afghanistan is that they can find a source of inspiration like my mother—one who will help pave the way for them to grow into strong women.

When Afghanistan became dangerous, just before the outbreak of the civil war in 1991, my family and I left the country as political refugees. We arrived in Germany without money or possessions. With three children in tow, the move was the most difficult step my parents had taken together. Because his medical qualifications were initially not recognized in Germany, my father worked as a flower salesman and later as a nurse. At first, it seemed fortunate for my mother that she was able to pursue her career any- where, without any additional exams or certifications. She kept working as a freelance journalist and wrote beautiful poems, but she was never able to read the news on TV again. During our first years in Germany, I remember my parents scraping together change from the government assistance cheques they had received to buy us kids ice cream.

Though the road to reclaim his career would be long, my father decided he wanted to work as a doctor again. With enormous ambition, he worked his way up. For a long time, he held an unpaid position as an assistant physician. It took him ten years, but the day he held a German medi- cal licence in his hands was the day my parents finally felt a sense of accomplishment.

But I do not want to promote the idea that refugees can do anything if they work hard enough. There will never be prosperity for my family like the prosperity other German families have built over generations, and I would not advise anyone to accept being exploited the way my father was when he worked without pay or security.

The challenges do not end for younger refugees either. Without speaking a word of German, I was enrolled in school at the age of five. Fortunately, I picked up the language quickly, and after school, I taught my sisters so that they would not have as hard a time in school as I did. Reading became my therapy, and it gave me access to the German language and culture that I needed in order to integrate. At least, I tried to integrate. Through it all, I encountered racism and never felt like I belonged anywhere. The road was rocky and meant many sacrifices for us as a family.

Despite the admiration I have for my father, I knew from the beginning that I wanted to follow in my mother's footsteps and become a journalist. Seeing her at work had a lasting impact on me. I knew even as a child that she could affect lives through her career, but I didn't understand the influence journalism would have on me until much later.

I still remember the day I travelled to Kabul for the first time after sixteen years away. I went to do empirical work for my final thesis in political science and media studies, which focused on the importance of media in Afghanistan's democratization process. Back then, at the end of 2008, there was still talk of a successful process. While the security situation had deteriorated again, both the Afghan government and the international community were putting out positive messages. They had said that the increasing number of Taliban attacks would quickly come to an end. By now we know that this was not the case.

Standing at a height of six feet, I often stood out in Germany. In Afghanistan, where the average height is much shorter because of decades of war and malnutrition, I stood out in any crowd. I was often perceived as a khareji (foreigner), but contrary to what I expected, I felt at home in Kabul. It felt as though I was reuniting with a childhood friend, and whatever time Kabul and I had spent apart was quickly forgotten. With questionnaires for my thesis research in hand, I walked from street to street, visiting the most eye-catching stores to begin my research. I was particularly interested to learn whether the Afghan media could make a positive contribution to the population's understanding of democracy in Kabul.

I had many conversations that led me to believe a diverse media landscape was enormously important to Afghans. Whether for information, education, or enter-tainment, television and radio were part of everyday life. Most homes and apartments in the capital had a tele-vision. Music could be heard everywhere. It was hard to believe that only eight years prior there had been no media except for the Taliban's propaganda stations. By 2008 this had changed explosively; there were about seventy TV stations, hundreds of radio stations, and dozens of newspapers. Billions of dollars were being pumped into Afghanistan, and much of it was invested in Afghan media. Journalists and media makers carefully built them up, continued their education, and learned more every day.

Compared to its neighbouring states, Afghanistan enjoyed a relatively free press until the Taliban takeover in August 2021. Although corruption and violence were normalized in the country, the media shaped an entire generation's understanding of its democratic structures. It also offered hope: hope for a strong democracy, participation, and self-determination. Despite the prevailing power relations, a diverse media landscape—consisting of private media, government media, NATO media, and Taliban media—made it possible for people to choose the information they absorbed and through which channels. This, in turn, allowed them to form their own opinions about issues. Media, I concluded, were among the strongest pillars of the fragile Afghan democracy.

In terms of holding the government to account, the media also performed an essential watchdog function. This is one of the reasons why I decided to become a journalist. With their growing professionalization, Afghan journalists had succeeded in reporting investigative stories and in denouncing grievances and corruption. They put their lives on the line for their work, and I admired them for it. One of the best examples of the health of the Afghan media landscape was the newspaper *Etilaat Roz*. With its award-winning investigative articles, it succeeded time and again in revealing public corruption scandals involving politicians. However, a few days after the Taliban took power, the paper was forced to stop printing for financial reasons and focused on its online work. To put an even finer point on how things have changed, before the Taliban took power in 2021, about one thousand Afghan women were journalists. A few days later, there were only about one hundred.

August 15, 2021, marked the beginning of a very difficult time for all Afghan media, but I remain convinced that with the help of what remains, especially social media, it is possible to significantly influence national political developments and the policies of the international community. Afghanistan is no longer a black box with no news getting in or out of the country, as it was in the 1990s. The last Taliban rule followed bloody years of civil war and decades of unrest. While there has still been a great deal of violence since 2001—about 47,000 innocent civilians have died—there have also been peaceful periods in parts of Afghanistan and positive developments for women who were able to pursue education and professions. Because of these achievements, I believe Afghans (both men and women) will not accept a Taliban rule like that of the 1990s. But time is running out, because eventually Afghanistan will disappear from the public conversation internationally and people will lose interest.

Does this mean the Taliban has adapted to people's expectations, or even changed? I believe the answer is no. The Taliban has shown that its ideology has not changed; the methods they are using are similar to those of two decades ago. They whip and beat people. Without due process, they execute alleged criminals, and they persecute minorities and critics. Women's social and professional lives are severely curtailed, and the press is massively restricted.

So, how can it be possible to work with the current Taliban regime in a solution-oriented way or even to try to bring about change? It will be the media, and especially social media, that will bring the actions of the Taliban and other militant groups from Afghanistan to the public. They are the link to the people on the ground and will ensure that they are not forgotten, even if the Taliban cuts off access to media.

I feel encouraged by the actions that people across the country are taking. Together with my colleagues, for example, I have tried to counter the cut-off by starting a shortwave radio program. Anyone with a suitable radio will be able to hear our broadcasts all over the country. Images of protesting women on the streets of Afghanistan also show us that Afghan women will by no means be content to stay in their homes. Many of these women are active on social media. They know that their images are seen abroad and that they have great international support. Together we will ensure the word gets out.

The power of the media, however, is a double-edged sword. The Taliban is also aware of its enormous influence, and Western journalists should be wary of falling into traps and playing into the hands of the Taliban. They often try to court Western journalists: they want to put forward a positive image so the new government will receive recognition and financial support. And sometimes foreign journalists are tempted by the adventure of talking to the Taliban, which was considered unreachable for many years.

CNN's chief international correspondent, Clarissa Ward, for example, tweeted that she felt she was witnessing history while wearing a full-face veil next to Taliban fighters. That moment may have been thrilling for her, but it (and moments like it) was a slap in the face for Afghan women journalists who fear for their lives and can no longer report. The work of Afghan journalists is obstructed on a daily basis. They get beaten and whipped. Reports of abductions are increasing. So it is not surprising that hundreds of Afghan journalists have fled, and those who are still in the country are self-censoring and/or hiding. This makes it all the more important that reporters who know Afghanistan well and speak the country's languages are supported abroad by Western governments and organizations. Free and independent reporting by Afghan media in exile is now more important than ever. They are the ones we should rely on to put as much pressure as possible on the militant Islamist group. With the help of funding, training, and lobbying, their work must be supported.

It's not only journalists who have left. Thousands of young Afghan hopefuls left the country after the fall of Kabul on August 15, 2021: artists, musicians, actors, photographers, human rights activists, journalists, athletes, scientists, and young government officials, both women and men, all looked for a way out. This mass exodus, and the accompanying "brain drain," is devastating to the country's human capital. In a Taliban-ruled Afghanistan, their absence leaves a huge void that will be felt at all levels, but especially in the sciences, research, and commerce. Nevertheless, representatives of this generation, many of whom are young enough that they did not experience the earlier years of Taliban oppression, continue the fight for peace and democracy in exile. To what extent they will be able to fight on the ground and have a future in their own country remains an open question.

But I believe in the flower that finds a way through the concrete. People will continue to seek out and produce art and culture. Women will continue to educate themselves and stand up for their rights. Human rights will not lose their validity, even now, and the democratic spirit, propagated by the West in Afghanistan (without, unfortunately, ever being sincerely implemented), will take an Afghan form. Even the Taliban will not be able to stop it.

In this new society, I hope that Afghan women will not be pushed to the margins of society, but that they will be central to the economic and social activities of Afghanistan. I hope all children will attend school. Child labourers and child soldiers must finally be things of the past. I hope that people will no longer go hungry and that children in particular will not suffer from malnutrition. But what I wish most for the Afghan people is that they can live self-determined lives free of violence.

For these hopes to become a reality, we must find ways to revive the Afghan economy and bring humanitarian aid to the country. And we must not recognize the Taliban as a legitimate government. Despite the need for Afghans to determine their own future, I do not want Afghanistan to be forgotten abroad. For twenty years, Western troops led by the United States occupied Afghanistan. And so I believe it continues to be the duty of the West to account for and come to terms with the mistakes made during that time, especially when it comes to the local forces that worked in service of the Western allies.

My assessment of the last twenty years, the last twelve of which I've spent working as a journalist, may seem somewhat disheartening. But I believe Afghan youth will not give up. And I hope that my work as a journalist will encourage other young Afghan women to get involved. Today I work at Deutsche Welle, where I am the first woman in the company's history to lead the Afghanistan editorial team—a team of almost forty colleagues.

My father spent a lifetime supporting his wife and daughters, and I know that today in Afghanistan there are other fathers like mine, with daughters they want to raise up but cannot because of the consequences they may face. The same is true for mothers like mine, who could enrich the country through their work in the media. This work would not only contribute to Afghan society by providing information on a large scale but would position them as positive public role models for future generations. Let us not force these women and girls and their male supporters into hiding or into exile. There is too much at stake.

MANIZHA WAFEQ

Manizha Wafeq is a gender and women's economic empowerment expert who advocates for women's businesses and gender equality in the private sector. She cofounded the Leading Entrepreneurs of Afghanistan for Development (LEAD), an advocacy platform for women's economic rights, which eventually led to the establishment of the Afghanistan Women Chamber of Commerce and Industry (AWCCI) in 2017. Through the Institute for Economic Empowerment of Women's (IEEW) Peace through Business program, she has trained and mentored over six hundred Afghan woman entrepreneurs from over seventeen provinces to establish and grow their businesses. She is a coauthor of the "Gender and the Legal Framework of Afghanistan" training manual; the founder of the Bibi Khadija Award, which honours successful businesswomen and role models in Afghanistan; and the winner of several awards for her advocacy and activism. She has an MBA from the American University of Afghanistan and a young daughter.

I WAS BORN in Kabul in 1985, the second of seven children. Both of my parents were military doctors and extraordinary people. My mother was an opinionated woman and was very proud to earn her own money and support her family. My father was a loving man with very tremendous affection for the world and its women and girls. They both loved children, and perhaps because of my father's wonderful attitude, God gave them five girls and two boys. He believed in humanity and considered his daughters as capable as his sons, so he made a great effort to raise them as strong, independent, and kind-hearted human beings who would put others first. Whenever a new daughter of his was born, my father would throw a festive celebration called a shab-e-shash, which was traditionally only held to observe the birth of a son.

I went to school in Shindand district, in Herat province, because both of my parents were transferred there when I was one and a half years old. We lived there for nine years. My parents stayed in Afghanistan during the Soviet-Afghan War (1979–1989) because they were both committed to serving their country; my sisters and I were able to continue going to school during that time. But when the Taliban took power in the mid-1990s and girls' schools were closed, my parents decided to leave the country. In 1995 we moved to Pakistan and didn't return until the Taliban was overthrown and an interim government was installed in 2002.

I was sixteen years old when we returned to Afghanistan and had just graduated from high school with a certificate in English and computer science. I immediately took a job and convinced my father that I should further my qualifications at the Kabul office of the Korea International Cooperation Agency (KOICA), a South Korean development aid organization. There I became the first female employee in a challenging work environment, and I relished the challenge to prove myself.

But I soon discovered that I was being paid less than my male colleagues for the same work. When I inquired about the disparity, I was told that the fieldwork the men did qualified them for higher pay. It didn't make sense to me. We had a lot of similar assignments: all of us accompanied our Korean colleagues to meetings and acted as translators, and we all went out to buy office equipment and handle travel logistics for the Afghan government delegations we sent to Korea.

However, there were also tasks, like dealing directly with contractors, that were not assigned to me. It seemed clear that they assumed a young woman would not be able to do that kind of work. But they didn't know that I had grown up in a home where my father had complete confidence in his daughters' abilities, and I really had not ever encountered sexism—at least not in that way. Over time, and through contact with other young Afghans who worked for different organizations, at workshops, or in the government, I realized that this behaviour had a name. It was discrimination against women and was defined by a lack of belief in women's abilities that grows from a gendered sense of superiority over women. This was unacceptable to me. I considered myself equal to men and even superior to some in certain ways.

My experience at KOICA drove me to shift my focus to women's empowerment and gender equality. In 2005 I changed careers: I took courses in gender studies and learned how Islam views gender equality. I was well trained and equipped with determination, and soon I took my skills to the battlefield. I became a gender equality trainer, joined women's movements, and empowered women with the belief that they were equally good or better than men in all spheres of life. The only thing getting in the way of women's excellence was the opportunities they were—or in many cases weren't—given.

But the lack of opportunities available in the past shouldn't determine a woman's future. I believe it is never too late to improve one's knowledge and skills or to help women take control of their own lives by helping them to get jobs, earn money, and become economically strong and independent.

In addition to working with women, I taught men who led departments in various government ministries

about the importance of weaving equitable gender prac-
tices into all of their activities and looking at their budgets
from a gender perspective to address inequality. It was
extremely satisfying to see them at least begin to think
about entrenched stereotypes and consider whether they
served girls, boys, men, and women equally well.

In 2007, I was selected for the Peace through Business
program offered by the U.S.-based nonprofit organization
Institute for Economic Empowerment of Women (IEEW),
and I was allowed to travel to the United States. There, we
were taught how to help build and grow businesses. I also
learned the importance of political advocacy for businesswomen. Dr. Terry Neese, founder and CEO of IEEW,
says it well: "If you are running a business and you are not
involved in politics, then politics will run your business."
In 2008 IEEW hired me as Afghanistan's country facilitator
and trainer. That year, I also started taking night classes
for an undergraduate science degree in economics, which
gave me a lot of important knowledge for working in the
economic sector. This year, 2022, is my fifteenth year of
training and mentoring businesswomen from around
Afghanistan, virtually this time: another twenty-five on
top of the six hundred who have already graduated.

After three cohorts of the program had graduated in
2009, we formed an alumni association, which we called
the Peace through Business Network. Our goal was to create a platform where we could continue to advocate for

the development of businesses. We wanted to support businesswomen and work to improve the business environment in Afghanistan, because policies did not have special provisions for women in business, offices were not women-friendly, and in general women were considered economic beneficiaries and not economic actors. We took that last idea, flipped it on its head, and turned it into our motto: "Afghan women are economic actors, not beneficiaries." It was important to set the record straight: women make up the majority of the producers of export commodities such as carpets, dried fruits, and valuable spices such as saffron. We knew that if women were acknowledged as economic actors, more consideration would be given to addressing their challenges.

In 2013, we felt the need to extend our reach further, and we met with a number of prominent woman entrepreneurs to discuss strategies for giving businesswomen in Afghanistan a platform, including one for political lobbying. We were supported by a number of inspiring mentors who had already established policy advocacy organizations in the United States, Sri Lanka, and Bangladesh. Thanks to their support and, of course, thanks to the IEEW, we were able to establish a women's chamber of commerce, adopt good bylaws, establish working governance models, and learn how to fund activities. Based on our learnings, eleven women formed a larger organization called Leading Entrepreneurs for Afghanistan's

Development (LEAD) in late 2013, which was officially launched on January 22, 2014.

In 2014, democratic presidential elections were held in Afghanistan for the third time. The runoff between Abdullah Abdullah and Ashraf Ghani that followed recounts and negotiations slowed our processes. Who became the next president would determine whether the ministers would remain in their posts. If new ministers came in, our lobbying efforts might have been wasted. That same year, International Security Assistance Force (ISAF) troops withdrew from Afghanistan, which caused a decrease of donations from the international community. In the absence of ISAF's soldiers in many areas, it was not possible to implement international development aid, and everything was put on hold—investments, buildings, and even marriages—as political instability and insecurity rose.

With so much uncertainty and instability, we decided to slow down and shift our efforts. We established an active research department and started to create a database of businesswomen. At the time, no one knew anything about how many of them there were, what kinds of businesses they ran, where they were located, or how many jobs they created. LEAD collected this basic data as well as information about the obstacles these businesswomen faced and the solutions they proposed. LEAD also conducted training to raise awareness about laws and regulations among businesswomen in Kabul and four other major provinces (Herat, Balkh, Nangarhar, and Kandahar) about the importance of and approaches to policy advocacy.

The year 2015 marked a breakthrough in my career. I decided to pursue my master's at the American University of Afghanistan while caring for my infant daughter. That same year, I founded an annual award to recognize successful Afghan businesswomen, naming it after the Prophet Mohammad's wife Khadija, who was the first Muslim female trader and philanthropist. Choosing this name was strategic: the Prophet worked for Khadija before they married each other. My hope was that the religious name of the award would serve as a reminder that women used to be involved in business—even the founding prophet of Islam worked for a woman. From 2015 to 2020, we recognized fifty businesswomen from over twenty provinces of Afghanistan, giving out awards that included $1,000 cash for business development purposes.

Meanwhile, LEAD's database on Afghan businesswomen was growing, and in 2016 it became part of an international conversation on the future of Afghanistan. We were able to provide the 2016 Brussels Conference on Afghanistan with statistics for discussion. If you don't know the facts or have statistics to share on an issue, it's difficult to have a meaningful conversation about it—or for it to become part of the conversation at all. I'm pleased to report that in 2016 the topic of Afghan women's economic empowerment became part of an international conference for the first time.

With its increased credibility, LEAD became the Afghanistan Women Chamber of Commerce and Industry (AWCCI), but not without overcoming some challenges. Representatives of the Afghanistan Chamber of Commerce and Industry (ACCI), which was the only existing chamber in the country at the time, tried to prevent us from gaining the approval of the High Economic Council, chaired by President Ashraf Ghani. But we had the support of First Lady Rula Ghani and were ultimately able to win the approval we longed for. The fly in the ointment was that our initial approval was granted for three years, during which time we had to prove we could run a successful operation. It was a day of mixed emotions. I felt happy about our victory, but I also felt the weight of responsibility as we considered how we would move forward.

After the official opening of the AWCCI and the election of new board members, we set up offices in the four major provinces—Herat in the west, Balkh in the north, Nangarhar in the east, and Kandahar in the south—and held board elections in all four regions. We proposed policy changes to the government and worked to secure a seat on the High Economic Council, the highest decision-making table. We organized a "buy from Afghan women's businesses" campaign, which included a policy provision that would give women a 5 percent preference in contract awards.

By December 2018—less than two years after the initial approval granted by the High Economic Council—we had already established five offices in Kabul and four zone offices, so we requested a meeting with President Ghani. We wanted to present our achievements and outline our future plans as a chamber of commerce to the president and first lady. President Ghani accepted our request, and the day we went to meet with him was a memorable one. There were thirty-five of us women (eleven board members from Kabul and five members from each of the other four offices, plus four staff). We were all feeling extremely happy, accomplished, and important because the president had accepted a meeting with us. After the meeting, the president again referred the matter to the High Economic Council for discussion, whereupon AWCCI's status as a permanent chamber was approved and enshrined in a presidential decree.

Before the Taliban seized control of the country on August 15, 2021, the public perception of businesswomen had improved and the reach of the AWCCI was immense at both the national and international levels. By that time, we had collected data that showed more than 2,471 licensed businesses and more than 54,000 unlicensed businesses were run by women. More than 130,000 jobs had been created, and many women were self-employed entrepreneurs. We were also being approached by media (both inside and outside of Afghanistan) and international organizations that wanted to learn how to promote women entrepreneurs. If our status as important business actors had not been accepted inside Afghanistan, we would not have been presented with these opportunities.

When I was asked to write this piece after the Taliban seized control of the country, I thought the progress we had made was already history. But I refuse to be defeated, because I have witnessed the progress women have achieved. They have established restaurants, travel agencies, export companies, IT and media service providers, logistics and construction companies, and much more over the past fifteen years. These women, with whom I met daily, are my source of energy, and I insist on continuing to view them as role models for the next generation of entrepreneurs. I remember Amena from Badakhshan, who started a successful dairy processing and packaging business. I see Nazifa from Parwan making fresh apple juice and packaging it in an environmentally friendly way. I remember how Marghuba in Kabul was still developing plans to expand her organic soap-making business through an online sales platform and to grow her farm. Many of the women I've met will remain in Afghanistan. Some did not want to leave the country, and others did not have the opportunity. And so AWCCI will continue to advocate for women business owners. The moment we lose hope, our long-standing efforts on behalf of Afghan businesswomen will also be undone, and I refuse to give away the confidence of over 57,000 women.

At the time of writing, it has been more than four months since Afghanistan was taken over by the Taliban for the second time. When professionals from all sectors left the country for fear of losing their lives, a great number of businesswomen, including AWCCI's chairperson, Afsana Rahimi, chose to remain to ensure women stay strong and stand for their right to continue to run their businesses. During this hard time, Rahimi has served as our role model for her patience, strength, and positivity. She mobilized businessmen and other male chamber leaders to highlight the existence of women's chambers and the importance of women's work in the private sector. We solicited the support of these men, and we will continue to do so. There are champions among them who stand with us to ensure we will be able to resume our work.

On October 31, 2021, the Afghanistan Chamber of Industries and Mines (ACIM) organized a business conference and exhibition to demonstrate the progress the sector has brought to Afghanistan and the important role it will play in resurrecting the economy, now more than ever. ACIM invited AWCCI's members, and around thirty businesswomen participated. They stood strong before their exhibition stalls and talked to the Taliban leaders. They proved that they are the new women of Afghanistan with more strength, resilience, and agency. They are not the women of the 1990s who submitted to the Taliban's demands to sit at home. Women in twelve provinces of the country that had previously hosted women's markets negotiated with the local Taliban to reopen their markets. They succeeded in being able to open shops and businesses that wouldn't have been allowed in the 1990s, including beauty salons. When people ask me if the Taliban has changed, I tell them it has not. It is our women who have changed.

Now that we are on a rapid downslope into economic and humanitarian crises in Afghanistan, there is an urgent need for continued support. Afghan businesswomen need to be set up with online sales platforms to help them sell their products to the world. We must continue educating them and advocating for them so that the current and next governments recognize the key role they play in the economic well-being of the community and the entire country. We need to ensure that Afghan women continue getting recognition for being economic *actors* and not *beneficiaries*!

MARIAM SAFI

Mariam Safi was born in Kabul in 1983. Her family left Afghanistan when she was five years old and immigrated to Canada. After studying political science and international peace studies, she returned to Kabul in 2007. In 2014, Safi founded the Organization for Policy Research and Development Studies (DROPS), a Kabul-based institute for research, community development, and women's empowerment. Her involvement in peacebuilding efforts included speaking to the United Nations Security Council. In January 2016, she was part of the Afghan delegation invited to Qatar for a two-day meeting with the Taliban political office. In 2014, Safi founded the peer-reviewed *Women and Public Policy Journal*, the first of its kind in Afghanistan, presenting articles by Afghan women on key national policy issues. She is considered one of the most distinguished experts in the fields of peace and conflict studies, community-based peacebuilding, and international interventions. She coauthored the 2022 scholarly work "Women and the Afghan Peace and Reintegration Process," published in *International Affairs*. Formerly a lecturer at the American

University of Afghanistan, she works with the United Nations, the European Union, NATO, and academic institutions in South Asia and North America.

———————

OVER THE PAST fifteen years, I have established myself as a researcher and peacebuilding practitioner with field experience in Afghanistan. For more than a decade I collated the perspectives of Afghans through consultations I led as part of our efforts at the Organization for Policy Research and Development Studies. But as the years went on, I realized how easily state actors overlooked these voices in favour of their own interests. Too often, they fell on deaf ears.

On August 15, 2021, after two decades of peacebuilding efforts, despair set in once again as the Taliban took over the country, including its capital, Kabul, and declared victory. What transpired on that day was a triumph of autocracy and the fall of democracy—facilitated in part by the sidelining of Afghan women during peacebuilding efforts and negotiations with the Taliban.

In 2001, Afghans had set off on a path towards a peaceful and stable future, one where they hoped conflict would become a distant memory. In the twenty intervening years, Afghanistan witnessed good progress. Women found representation in all sectors of Afghan society, a vibrant new generation of youth emerged, and a promising, if shaky, democratic system of governance had been established. It was all made possible because Afghans welcomed international investment and commitments to support the hope for a peaceful future.

The gains in Afghanistan were largely an outcome of the hopes that locals held in response to promises that came with the international peacebuilding agenda. Most academics and practitioners understand *peacebuilding* as measures to consolidate peace and advance a sense of confidence and well-being among people. Creating a liberal peace became the goal of most efforts in Afghanistan post-2001. Afghans held to the belief that state actors would achieve positive peace by placing those who were previously sidelined—namely local actors, women, minority groups, and civil society—at the centre of their peacebuilding efforts.

In 2018 I was invited to speak to the United Nations Security Council (UNSC) on International Women's Day. I believed there would be no greater platform to raise the perspectives and concerns of Afghans—in particular those of women—and to invoke a real shift in the perception of where Afghanistan was and where it was going, so I agreed to go. In my speech, I explained, "Seventeen years ago, hope replaced despair, and Afghans embarked on the path towards a peaceful and stable future where conflict would become a distant memory. We welcomed the international investment and commitment to support this hope." But I also cautioned the UNSC that the hope for continued and sustained peacebuilding was beginning to fade. While international partners repeatedly expressed their intention and will to stand behind the people of Afghanistan to bring lasting peace, security, and stability, it was time to stand *beside* them. There was a crucial need for the international community to shoulder the responsibilities of state-building instead of cutting their losses and hiding behind the guise of a transition to local ownership. After all, the state-building process Afghanistan was engaged in was built upon Western blueprints.

When the U.S. began to negotiate with the Taliban in 2018, Afghan women and civil society asserted themselves to preserve the gains that had been made in previous years. It was around this time that the international peacebuilding efforts really lost steam. War-weary and frustrated, the U.S. and its NATO allies decided a military victory against the Taliban was not in the cards. To save face, they pursued an agreement with the Taliban. Throughout this process, the Afghan state and its citizens were excluded. Instead, they freed thousands of Taliban prisoners, conditioned solely on the Taliban promise that Afghan territory would not be used by militant groups against America's interests.

In September 2019, I urged another UN body, the United Nations General Assembly (UNGA), to recognize the trajectory it was on and change its course. Without a significant change in strategy, the international community and its Afghan partners risked a monumental loss of rights for all Afghans after eighteen years of gains. Their peacebuilding intervention would be a failure.

The role of women in peacemaking had proven to be significant, yet Afghan women and civil society actors were constantly relegated to the margins. During the U.S.-Taliban peace deal negotiations, civil society and women's groups told U.S. Special Representative for Afghanistan Reconciliation Zalmay Khalilzad that issues such as human rights, women's rights, social justice, and protection of the constitution should be red lines. They were values the U.S. and Afghanistan had worked together to build. However, the U.S. often left these issues out of its negotiations with the Taliban. In particular, views expressed by women were segregated from so-called hardline issues, such as peacemaking and troop withdrawal, and instead treated as "women's issues."

It is worth noting that opinions differed in Afghanistan both between and among different groups, including women, on the type of peace that should unfold. And while there should have been more respect and acknowledgement of the differences in the opinions of these women, mounting pressures from the international community made them realize quickly that developing a unified platform was the only way they could ensure women's voices would be at the negotiating table. While that was incredibly disheartening, it is notable that women were able to pull together and reach a consensus while men's opinions were often discussed in all of their contradictions.

Unfortunately, steps to achieve their proposed peace were never taken, at least not while the U.S. negotiated its deal with the Taliban or as far as an "Afghan Peace Process" is concerned. It turned out the space for women to voice their opinions did not exist.

And yet there was continued mobilization among women and women's organizations. This only under-scored the fact that women in Afghanistan were able to come together in ways never before witnessed in any peace process around the world. Their advocacy was quick and cut across ethnic, religious, and sectorial lines with a clear goal: to make sure civil liberties, democracy, and women's constitutional rights were not eroded. They held nationwide consultations, talked with current and former Taliban members, organized conferences and roundtables, wrote op-eds, carried out peaceful protests in Kabul and around the country, and provided policy rec-ommendations in publications such as the DROPS *Women and Public Policy Journal.*

Afghan women also called upon the international com-munity to stand with them in their fight for inclusion and sustainable peace. #NoPeaceWithoutWomen, #MyRedLine, and #WomenWillNotGoBack are only some of the mes-sages that spread across social media. The message was loud and clear: any process that leaves women behind is not only unacceptable but also doomed to fail.

In undermining women's legitimacy, the international community offered de facto legitimacy to the Taliban. The Taliban was implicitly portrayed as "local," which gave it agency to shape the peace agreement, despite continuing to kill scores of innocent Afghans. Meanwhile, women and their organizations were treated as "spoilers." When women demanded their constitutional rights be preserved, they were shushed and told by the international community that such issues were outside the prerogative of the peace talks. When they cautioned against quick fixes, women were criticized for not taking ownership of their future.

Any hope for peace between the Afghan state and the Taliban died when the latter took over the country. While all parties, including the Taliban, urged a political solution as the most desirable means to end the conflict in Afghanistan, a military approach became the ultimate solution for the Taliban.

In short, the Taliban victory was the outcome of twenty years of contradictory strategies by Western allies and their Afghan patrons. The pursuit of peacebuilding, which was being undertaken in the background of elite-led state-building and counterinsurgency efforts, had grave costs for Afghans:, it created a highly fragile foundation for economic development, stability, and peace to take root.

These are the pitfalls of liberal peacebuilding: when it matters most, those in positions of power adopt unliberal approaches and justify them through the promise of liberal outcomes.

Even though the Taliban committed to a code of conduct that would protect civilians during the peace talks, the group continued to carry out attacks in densely populated areas, showing no regard for civilian lives. The Taliban also began targeting women activists, civil society actors, journalists, and religious scholars. There was a rise in civilian casualties, particularly among women and children (which rose the highest), followed by a number of internally displaced people and asylum seekers. In the first half of 2021, the United Nations Assistance Mission in Afghanistan (UNAMA) documented 5,183 civilian casualties, a 47 percent increase compared with the same period in 2020. The most shocking aspect of this figure is that women and children made up close to half of all civilian casualties in the first half of 2021. Comprising 46 percent of all civilian casualties, 32 percent were children and 14 percent were women. UNAMA reported that more women and children had been killed and injured in the first half of 2021 than ever before.

Despite Afghans losing hope in the latter years of the Islamic Republic, they remained hopeful about democracy. The mobilization of women's groups and civil society actors witnessed in these years was a testament to this.

I still believe what I told the UNGA: that the time has come to apply the lessons we have learned about peacebuilding and to place local communities, particularly women and civil society, at the centre of efforts to resolve conflict. That is the only way to achieve a peace that lasts. We must bring these values to our peacebuilding work in Afghanistan. Now, as we face a new reality in the country, we must reflect on these ideas, hold ourselves accountable for where we have landed, and commit ourselves to not repeating those mistakes.

ROYA SADAT

Born in Herat in 1983, Roya Sadat is one of Afghanistan's most prominent filmmakers and focuses on Afghan women in her documentaries and feature films. Her first screenplay was written during the Taliban era (1996–2001), when she and her five sisters were no longer allowed to go to school and were taught by their mother at home. In 2003, she made her first film, *Se noghta* (*Three Dots*), which won numerous awards. The same year, she founded Roya Film House, Afghanistan's first film production company founded by women. In 2017, she released *Namai ba rahis gomhor* (*A Letter to the President*). She is the cofounder and vice president of the Herat International Women's Film Festival. In 2018, she received the International Women of Courage Award. In addition to making the BBC's list of "100 Women of 2021," Sadat was also awarded the prestigious Kim Dae Jung Nobel Peace Film Award as part of the International Peace Film Festival in December 2021. She was recognized for her work promoting democracy, human rights, and peace through film, and for her socially critical films that raise important human rights issues.

(The following interview was conducted by Nahid Sha-halimi in October 2021.)

———————————

In your films, you tell stories of Afghan women. What do you think makes Afghan women special?

Afghan women, whether in the fields of art, culture, politics, or otherwise, have fought for their rights more than other women in the world, because there have been and still are so many obstacles and winding paths in front of them. Making art, in particular, is still a social taboo in Afghanistan, an unacceptable field of employment for women. However, women always try to use their knowledge, experience, and assertiveness to advance in society. Afghan women should be judged based on their persistent skills and talents. In my view, a person's mindset is more important than their background or gender—and that is also a central theme in my cinematic work.

How did you become a filmmaker?

My mother's stories and the mythological tales I heard as a child sparked my interest in literature, encouraged playwriting as a teenager, and led me to storytelling in my subconscious. Throughout my life of facing injustice and inequality, I realized more and more that cinema and filmmaking gave me a voice. Making films is my life, and it is the birthplace of thought for me.

My father was a respected man who, like many men, wanted to have a boy as his first child. In his opinion, the combination of abilities, passion, and talent could only be reflected in a boy. Unfortunately, this misconception prevailed in my family. As a result, my sisters and I tried to be twice as good as the boys. Today, all of my sisters work in various fields of art and culture. When my father saw our talents and abilities, he recognized them, and from then on, he helped and supported us in all areas of our lives.

What is your intention with your films, and what do you hope to achieve with them?

First of all, I think the world has become accustomed to Afghanistan's tragedies, but I don't want Afghanistan to always be seen as the site of tragedy—or for its women to be seen as victims. Our work is all about women. Women are the protagonists. We also hold workshops to familiarize women with filmmaking techniques.

At the International Women's Film Festival of Afghanistan, which started in 2013, we made it clear that our main concern is to focus on women's stories. We want to show women in our society as individuals whose work and intelligence are needed, rather than continuing to show women only as symbols of gender discrimination. Through the films and our related work, Afghans' views on the film industry have changed. In the early days, few were willing to let their daughters work in the film industry, but now many parents are enthusiastic about their daughters working in film. Our work has increased people's confidence in the field. In 2021, we were planning to hold the festival for the seventh time.

How much do your portrayals of female characters reflect you?

I believe that the characters in my films were influenced by different processes of consciousness. The characters from my first films, then later in the TV series and subsequent works, have gone through different stages of development. For example, the protagonist of the film *Three Dots* [2003] is still a silent heroine, while in the film *A Letter to the President* [2017], the main character is rebellious. And, of course, each film has its own narrative structure and effect.

Since 2003, you have been involved with the Afghan film industry in a variety of ways. What do you wish for the future of Afghan film and for yourself?

Unfortunately, arts and culture have never been taken seriously at the government level in Afghanistan. Our repeated efforts with the Ministry of Information and Culture were always rejected because of lack of funding. The ministers of Information and Culture have been more interested in social relations over the last twenty years. Art has not been their concern. The government has not supported the film industry, and the lack of security in the country has prevented international producers from investing in Afghanistan. For these reasons, it has been very difficult for film production companies to survive.

Despite the political and social pressures we have experienced at different times, we have tried to produce impactful results for society. We must continue to tell stories. Movies and cinema illustrate history.

My hope is that we will be able to speak and create art about the current situation in the country without every word and work being censored. That may result in no one daring to produce anything. I also hope young female filmmakers will try to establish themselves in international film markets. And as for women in the film sector in Afghanistan, every single effort they make in the film industry is valuable. We have promoted and supported women's films through our own company and with film festivals—and we will continue to promote women.

We have made many sacrifices in these twenty years; we have worked hard. My generation helped build a society from the ground up—and now we have lost it all again.

However, there must be hope! The situation must not remain like this! We will achieve change again and a civilized society that strives for freedom, justice, and equality. I have dedicated my whole life to the art of filmmaking and cinema. I hope to return home soon and continue my work. The world has a responsibility to us, but right now it seems that it has nothing to say. Our only choice at the moment is to motivate ourselves and not lose hope!

HILA LIMAR

Hila Limar was born in Afghanistan in 1986 and fled to Germany with her parents and siblings in 1990. She is an architect and the chairwoman of the board of Visions for Children in Hamburg, a nonprofit organization that aims to improve learning conditions in schools and educational quality in regions of poverty, crisis, and war.

ا ب پ ≈ ABC . . . These simple letters cannot be read by 70.2 percent of women in Afghanistan. The armed conflicts, ongoing for over four decades, have had an immense impact on educational justice, and Afghanistan has become the country with the largest gender gap in access to education.

There is a structural shortage in education due to a lack of schools and teaching staff. Then there are fears of attacks—kidnappings, beatings, sexual assaults—being launched at children while they travel to school. All of these factors make girls less likely to attend school. In rural areas, traditional norms and economic challenges keep girls out of school as well. Daughters are required to do household chores, perform childcare, or work in the fields. Schooling is perceived to be of no benefit to these activities. The economic challenges combined with patriarchal tribal structures often push girls to marry at an early age, before they've completed a basic education. All of this promotes and maintains injustice and inequality in education.

So what are the consequences if 2.2 million girls—or 60 percent of all primary-school-aged children—cannot attend school? The fact of the matter is that they are being denied a human right and the possibility of leading a self-determined life. Each year of secondary schooling a young girl completes reduces her chance of early marriage (at an age under eighteen). Based on the many conversations I've had with girls in Afghanistan and knowledge accumulated by various NGOs, marriage at a very young age can even have fatal consequences for girls: not only does it force them to abandon any educational opportunities, but their bodies may not be mature enough to handle a pregnancy. Early marriage and pregnancy often lead to physical stress and psychological trauma that some girls never overcome. It may also limit their ability to pursue gainful employment, which is already difficult for women because of the dire security situation and male-dominated society. The stakes are even higher when you consider that, globally, a woman's earnings can increase by up to 20 percent for every additional year of schooling she completes as a girl. In countries like Afghanistan, even a simple primary school diploma can lift people out of the deepest poverty. Their education plays a decisive role not just in their own lives but in shaping society as a whole.

If my parents had not fled from Afghanistan to Germany, I too would have been one of those uneducated girls. My education almost certainly would have ended in 1996, in the fourth grade, with the invasion of the Taliban. When they came to power, girls and women were excluded from public life, including the school system.

As victims of war living in Germany, we had to deal with new challenges, but at least our basic needs and our human rights were met. Over the years, I have come to appreciate my ability to go to school more and more. My high school diploma, for example, not only opened up opportunities for my professional career but also paved the foundation for my self-confident, independent, and critical approach to the world. Each and every year of basic schooling and my subsequent studies significantly shaped my political engagement, my understanding of justice, and my mental and physical health.

At university, while studying architecture, I met the founders of Visions for Children, a nonprofit organization that aims to improve the learning conditions for children in conflict and war zones. At that time, the organization consisted of a small circle of friends who supported a school in Kabul. Their desire to help Afghan children by providing quality education, initially through infrastructure and later through workshops and trainings, moved me to join in their efforts.

As I engaged more deeply in this work, my desire to visit the school project in Afghanistan grew. Stories told by my family—and especially by my parents—had already piqued my interest. I was intrigued by the few photos my parents had been able to save during their escape from Afghanistan. The images were precious, and their stories kept memories of their homeland alive. Despite the nostalgia, sadness, and sometimes even brutal memories they had, they would always say things like "Afghanistan has the most beautiful landscape and the most imposing mountains in the world," or "In Afghanistan, we felt understood and taken care of." I wanted to experience the country for myself.

Knowing that, on average, a child has died in Afghanistan every five hours over the past twenty years, and that it makes the country one of the most dangerous places in the world, did not slow me down. This danger—or, rather, emergency—only increased my motivation to go there. I wanted to know what it would feel like to actually put my feet on the ground in Afghanistan. At the same time, I was worried that I might not experience the country my parents had described. I was worried that I would feel like a foreigner who did not belong.

But then, finally, the day arrived—and the moment I flew over Afghanistan for the first time, the incredible panorama of the Hindukush Mountains just overwhelmed me: snow-covered and bright white, green, and brown. Every few minutes the landscape offered a new spectacle. I felt an inner peace, and my skepticism concerning my parents' descriptions evaporated with every minute I spent contemplating the land passing by below me. I was mesmerized by its beauty. Tears came to my eyes as we approached Kabul, and before I even set foot on the ground, I felt deeply connected to the city, the country, and its people.

As it was then, it has been the case ever since. An essential part of my travelling to Afghanistan relates, of course, to my work for Visions for Children. When I go there, I meet with school management, the student body, the teachers, and the parents of the students.

On my first trip to the country, I visited one of our school projects in Khoja Boghra, close to Kabul Airport, where there weren't enough classrooms. Classes were held partly in a ruinous building, partly in a neighbouring building in need of renovation, and even outdoors. When I entered the school grounds for the first time, I did not see any students, but I heard a lot of voices. I naively asked, "Is it recess?" The principal replied, "No. Why?" As we turned the corner, the rest of the schoolyard came into view and I realized the reason for the loudness. What

I had heard were the voices of many hundred students, all of them being taught outside while sitting on the ground in 35 degree Celsius weather.

Every time I visit a school, I ask the children the same questions to better understand their situation: "Are there other schools in the neighbourhood?" "Yes." "Do the children there also have their classes outside?" "No." "Is there anything you wish was different about your school?" "No." When I ask how they are doing and if they are lacking anything, most children appear overwhelmed. They know nothing but war; they and their families struggle to survive every day. Being allowed to go to school, perhaps as one of many children in their family, is a great privilege for them. The intimate conversations I have in smaller groups or in one-on-one situations help me to better understand everyday life on site and the challenges and needs associated with it. Making demands of the teachers or the school infrastructure would never cross their minds. But after a while, they warm up and gain the confidence to tell me their desires: new classrooms, a new library, and washrooms. I am always struck by how reserved the girls are in responding to my questions, even if they are not at all personal or technical but merely concerned with the needs of the school.

Girls attending school are often more self-confident than they would be otherwise. They are proud of being able to learn, and they are particularly hardworking.

I have made this observation on every project trip so far, at each one of our schools. Girls in Afghanistan grow up completely differently than girls in Germany and other, higher-income countries. At a young age, they are burdened with many obligations: they bear the responsibility for their siblings and their household; they often work cultivating land; and they are indispensable to the financial well-being of their families. Many of them have told me that they go to school because it's one of the few things they can do just for themselves. At school they find the space and opportunity to learn and grow personally.

I first met the girls from the school in Khoja Boghra at the inauguration of the new building we had constructed together and then a second time months later. After settling into their new environment, I found that they had changed notably. They indeed had blossomed and had become more motivated and self-confident in their aspirations and goals. On my second visit, I had a conversation with a grade-eleven student named Samira that I remember vividly and that still lingers inside me:

SAMIRA: Are you here with your husband?
HILA: I'm not married.
SAMIRA: How old are you?
HILA: Thirty-two.
SAMIRA (ASTONISHED): Okay. And your parents allow you to travel alone?

HILA: They don't want me to travel to Afghanistan at all because they hear about all of the attacks in the news. It makes no difference to them if I'm alone or if I'm accompanied by someone. But I think it's important that I'm here, that you get to know me, and that I get to know you. Together we can change things.

SAMIRA: Tell your parents not to worry. You are standing up for us and other girls and boys here and our prayers will always protect you.

I had not been questioned like that before, and I wasn't sure if my honesty was appropriate or if it might have left a negative impression. The reactions of the girls in the class were troubling. Their irritation and curiosity about my presence as a young Afghan woman who had come all the way from Germany seemed palpable. In the hallway afterwards, I met a teacher and told her about the conversation. I told her about my impression, that I might have been met with a lack of understanding and that I would be very sorry if the school were to get in trouble because the girls went home and told their parents that "yak dukhtar as alman amada, tanha, be shawhar, be madar ya padar, wa mekhoya ke komak kuna" (a girl from Germany is here, alone, without husband or parents, and she wants to support us). I could already hear the parents' discontented responses: "We don't want such a person. We don't need her help." Once again, I apologized and hoped that my openness would not jeopardize the school's position.

During another visit a few days later, the teacher told me that it had been right to be honest: "The students haven't met an Afghan woman like you before. It has shown them a new perspective: that they don't have to get married immediately after graduating high school. They now see that it's possible to study instead and continue their education." Education strengthens not only the future prospects of girls and young women but also their self-confidence, and it's a real joy to see that.

Anyone who had anything to do with Afghanistan was anxiously anticipating September 11, 2021, the historic date by which President Biden had announced he intended to withdraw all U.S. troops from the country. Both he and the rest of the international community left the question of what would come after unanswered.

It is probably human nature to hope that such an uncertain day will never come. Instead, it arrived sooner than expected, in mid-August. As one city after another fell into the hands of the Taliban, it became the new political authority in the country.

During the last fifteen years, we at Visions for Children have worked to create a safer Afghanistan with freedom and opportunities for women and girls. We have built seven schools and reached a total of about fifteen thousand children. All of that is now in danger of falling apart. The shock, anger, and powerlessness make it difficult to move, to breathe, and to be. We are grieving. I often wonder what stage of grief we are in. Is it denial, anger, bargaining, depression, acceptance? When will we be able to move on? Because we have to. We must act and move on. There is a responsibility to our colleagues and family members, to our friends, and, of course, to all the students and their families. To all those who are still in Afghanistan, I ask, How are our colleagues doing? What will happen to our projects? What can we do from outside the country? How do we deal with the Taliban? It is still too early to answer these questions, but they must be answered as soon as possible. What is clear, however, is that we, as a nongovernmental organization with many partners on site, are staying in Afghanistan. We will, one way or another, continue our work and cooperation for the benefit of education, justice, and freedom.

The task now is to ensure and reinforce the successes and achievements made so far. Our efforts must not be in vain. At the same time, we have to continue our campaign in order to strengthen the value of education as a fundamental human right and as a basic tool for securing peace and gender equality.

Between 2001 and 2021, the school enrollment rate in Afghanistan increased almost tenfold, according to UNESCO, and the number of schools rose from 3,400 to 16,400. Ninety percent of girls and 94 percent of boys who attend secondary school (grades seven to twelve) complete their lower secondary (grades seven to nine) education. The effects of their education extend well beyond themselves, reaching their siblings, parents, friends, and neighbours. However, an average of 45 percent of children (3.7 million) still do not attend school nationwide. This particularly affects girls.

In half of the country's provinces, less than 20 percent of teachers are women. This presents a hurdle for girls whose families will not allow them to be taught by men. Moreover, educational institutions remain particularly dangerous places. Routes to school are often dangerous, susceptible to assaults, and in bad condition, and attacks on schools have also increased. Between 2017 and 2018, they tripled, and by the end of 2018, more than one thousand schools were closed because of constant armed conflict and the political situation in the country.

The relationship between education and the military-political conflict is mutually dependent. Numerous examples show that if young people don't go to school and/or are given unequal educational opportunities, societies become more vulnerable to situations of conflict and fragmentation. Without education, young people are more likely to go down a road towards poverty and unemployment, which, in turn, increases the likelihood that those affected will join armed militias. At the same time, conflict prevents infrastructure from being sustained and developed, which impedes access to schooling. In this kind of situation, a strong education system is needed to break the feedback loop.

Germany is the second largest donor to Afghanistan after the United States. Visions for Children's projects are also funded by the German government. In our view, Germany has to take responsibility for Afghanistan's future and for safeguarding the successes of the past twenty years. This means Germany must continue to work for and with the people in Afghanistan, but it also has to reflect on its intentions, actions, and impact on the Afghanistan mission.

A meta-review by Germany's Federal Ministry for Economic Cooperation and Development illustrates the impact of small NGOs in development cooperation. The report clearly states that, despite large-scale projects in Afghanistan, the international community's approach to development cooperation has not paid sufficient attention to the desires, needs, opportunities, and capacities of civil society. Grassroots projects or grassroots and civil initiatives that work and organize closely with or from within local communities and take into account their needs pave the way for sustainable development and cooperation. These observations confirm our on-the-ground experiences in cooperation and show that we were already on the right track. However, the hasty withdrawal of U.S. soldiers without developing a contingency plan for civil society, the failed evacuation, and the fact that funding for education projects has been stopped has gradually made the position of the German government clear. Germany apparently no longer has any interest in sustainable and long-lasting cooperation with the Afghan civilian population.

For a long time, I kept the decisions of the German government to myself and did not share them with our colleagues in Afghanistan. I worried how my colleagues would react. They already felt betrayed after the failed evacuation, and now the work they are doing is being doubted. The fact that this decision is political and not personal is of no interest at the moment. We keep stating the urgency of the current situation, we continue to propose actions and projects, but the official and almost automatic answers from the ministries are empty words of diplomacy: "We are thinking about it. We have taken note of it."

However, "thinking about it" is not enough. We have to act now and treat this like the emergency it is. Among other things, we must continue our educational work on the ground and keep our educational goals in mind, even under these catastrophic circumstances. Education is not negotiable. Education is a fundamental human right. And it is our responsibility to set an example here and now: we will not leave you, the children of Afghanistan, alone; we will continue our work.

FAWZIA KOOFI

Born in 1975 in the northeastern Afghan province of Badakhshan, Fawzia Koofi studied law, political science, and international relations. She was a member of parliament and chairwoman of the Committee on Women and Human Rights. From 2005 to 2019, she was the first vice president of the National Assembly. To ensure that she could not pose a threat to Ashraf Ghani as a challenger in the 2014 presidential elections, the age for presidential candidacy was raised to forty. She has been an advocate for women prisoners, women and children who have suffered from violence, access to education, and more. She is chairwoman of the Movement of Change for Afghanistan party and was one of four women who participated in the 2020 peace negotiations with the Taliban in Doha. In 2020, she was nominated for the Nobel Peace Prize. She is the author of the bestselling memoir *The Favored Daughter*. (The following interview was conducted by Nahid Shahalimi in September 2021.)

Are you still in Afghanistan, now that the Taliban has taken power?

I am currently in Doha, Qatar, because I had to flee Afghanistan to protect my family and myself. I have spent my whole life in Afghanistan. Only in the last year have I been shuttling back and forth between Afghanistan and Doha, because that is where we were negotiating with the Taliban. Otherwise, my life, my family, my house, my political activity are in Afghanistan.

I have never actually considered leaving the country. Throughout the years and through everything that has happened in Afghanistan—that is, every regime change— my life and the lives of millions of other Afghans have been completely changed. We have lost our homes, our opportunities for education, our jobs, just everything. But I never thought of leaving, because I always believed that we could change things from within. We have to change within the system. However, because of the many uncertainties and the lack of security, many talented and well-educated Afghans have left the country—that was never my plan and I hope to return.

What challenges have you faced as a female parliamentarian?

Being a working woman is not easy in any part of the world, whether as a politician or in any other profession. In a country like Afghanistan, where the entire administration had collapsed during the civil war, we had to deal with the extreme interpretations of Islam during the Taliban regime. Nevertheless, there was an opportunity for women after 2001. Under the constitution, women could run for parliament.

Since my father had been a respected member of parliament (he was killed during the Soviet intervention while he was on a peace mission), people voted for me. That made me happy, but I saw an even greater task in fighting for and with women on my own. So, in 2005 I decided to run for deputy speaker of the House of Representatives to represent the voices of Afghan women who had not been heard before. In the first round of my candidacy, people talked about how I dressed, who I talked to, what my scarves looked like, and whether I wore lipstick. However, when people realized my potential and perseverance, they stopped focusing on my appearance. In the end, I was elected vice president of the parliament.

The next challenge for me was to pass laws to protect women. I fought for more participation for women in the peace process, because when I first met with the Taliban in Doha, I was shocked to be the only woman at the table. In the end, there were three other women involved in the peace negotiations.

What issues were discussed during the peace negotiations?

There were many issues—from human rights to the Islamic rights of women—but it was difficult to negotiate with the Taliban because it was bringing religion into any discussion. For example, there was also the issue of how to preserve our cultural heritage, which included the sites of the (destroyed) Buddhas in Bamiyan and other cultural sites in the country. The Taliban demanded that we destroy anything that contradicts Islam.

In the last twenty years, there have been several violent physical attacks on you. How have you dealt with the burdens and challenges associated with them?

Certainly, it is a great burden, but I don't consider it as my personal challenge, because not only was I attacked, but numerous people in the country were attacked and killed as well. The country has lost many of its intellectuals and talents. We all have loved ones to mourn. I lost my father, my brothers, and my husband in this war. I want to spare other people these losses. I want political solutions. I want elections instead of weapons.

There was one attack in 2010 that was particularly difficult for me to deal with. I was invited to an International Women's Day celebration in Nangarhar, a good two hundred kilometres east of Kabul. When I drove back the next day, we were on a very rocky road when the first bullet was fired. The echo in the mountains was so strong that it took us a moment to understand where the bullets were coming from. My daughters and my sisters were also in the car with me. The bullets were meant for us. My sister pushed my head under the seat to protect me. We backed up and our people started shooting back. When we were going so fast that the driver almost lost control of the vehicle, I sat up and talked to him to calm him down. I didn't want to die in a car accident. After about forty minutes, we reached a small tunnel and waited there. Finally, I was evacuated to Kabul. This attack was especially difficult for me because I was worried not only for my own safety but also for the lives of everyone else in the car with me.

Unfortunately, concern for one's own life and the lives of loved ones is not uncommon for the Afghan community. Almost everyone who was in an exposed position as a public figure was and is threatened. The attack in August 2020 left my right hand injured, and it is still less functional, but that gave me even more reason to represent victims of war in the peace negotiations.

What do you think is the best way to negotiate with the Taliban regime?

I think there are some issues on which they are more open to change. However, negotiating may be even more difficult this time, due to the fact that the Taliban is now in power and there is no political pressure that can be applied by the international community. Although the Taliban is not willing to discuss changing its core values, which include the Islamic rights of women and the destruction of anything that is not Islamic, it is important to negotiate.

What will happen to the so-called Freedom Generation that came of age in the early 2000s?

It is upsetting to see that those who have fled the country are those in whom the country has invested the most, such as skilled workers, journalists, artists, actors, and others. It will take the country decades to bring back these talents and intellectuals. I think those who are still in Afghanistan have a choice to make. Either they live under the repressive measures and accept that many years of deprivation will lie ahead, or they move forward. Moving forward will certainly require struggle and sacrifice. People have to be willing to take that on, and I'm sure they will.

What are your plans for the future?

My goal is to provide more opportunities for women to use their skills and knowledge to lead others and fight for their rights. In any case, I will continue to try to educate and empower the nation and encourage women to stand up for their rights. I hope that in five years, or sooner, I will see a woman representing the people and the nation in a leadership position.

HOSNA JALIL

Born in Ghazni in southeastern Afghanistan in 1992, Hosna Jalil studied physics and business administration. She was appointed deputy minister of Interior Affairs at the age of twenty-six and was later appointed minister of Women's Affairs. As the first woman to hold such a high-ranking security position, her responsibilities included increasing the participation of women in the police force. She currently lives in the United States, where she is pursuing a degree in strategic security studies. Her goal is to return to Afghanistan and change the country from within.

THE FIRST YEARS of my life were lived in the immediate aftermath of the civil war, and most of my childhood was governed by the Taliban regime. When they were driven out in December 2001, I was nine and a half years old. After that, the best time of my life began.

In a society where every decision about my life was made by the male members of my family, I decided to choose my own last name at the age of thirteen, and I chose my father's first name. In Afghanistan, women are saddled with many obligations, constraints, and expectations. Choosing my own name gave me a sense of independence and individuality, without separating me from my family. It was a step I took to build my identity and decide who I wanted to be.

I had always wanted to be independent and self-reliant. As I grew older, it became important to me that I, and all of the other women in Afghanistan, could access the opportunities that men in our country enjoy as a matter of course. I wanted to take action against the restrictions women in our country faced so that other women and future generations would be able to reach their full potential. My dream was to one day hold a position where I could make a difference for all Afghans. I was fully aware that a lot of criticism would accompany me in such a significant role, but I wanted to lead others so we could make progress together.

My professional career began in the private sector, where I pursued many different opportunities. But there was a common thread that ran through each new challenge I took on: I wanted to get out of my comfort zone and find my way in a new environment.

In 2015, when I was eager to explore a new working environment and different sets of challenges, a short-term position in the president's economic advisory office was announced. I had a negative image of the government and its bureaucracies that had been shaped by working in the private sector, but I applied for the opening anyway. I wanted to see for myself how the government functioned. After the contract ended in December 2015, I worked in the private sector for another two years; in 2018, I returned to the government. I had the passion, commitment, and belief that I could help to create positive change from inside the government that would benefit the private sector and the Afghan people. Corruption in Afghan politics takes many forms, and government interference in the affairs of NGOs and the private sector is a big challenge. Despite the dangers of getting involved from the inside, I wanted to find ways to bring in rules that set clear boundaries for government engagement and effected change.

From there, I continued to move within the government. When I joined Afghanistan's security sector in the leading role of deputy minister of Interior Affairs, I made it my goal, on behalf of all girls and women, to demonstrate that there's no such thing as a "manly" or male-only profession. I wanted them to dream of doing what they enjoyed and what they could potentially be good at, not what our male-dominated society thought was good for them.

Being in politics is difficult everywhere. Every country has its own challenges. But Afghanistan is one of the few countries where assassinations and personal attacks on politicians occur so frequently that they seem a normal part of political life. From the beginning, I was not taken seriously and was made to feel like I did not belong in politics. It was hard not to be discouraged by the rejection, and I paid a heavy price for my new position. For the first time, my ethical principles were questioned in the media—not just by the general public but by people I knew. Members of parliament and pundits would point to me as one of the government's biggest failures when it came to appointing ministers; daily social media scandals emerged and were subsequently dissected by national print media outlets. Many claimed that I, and other women in the government, had only received our positions in return for sexual favours. The more important the position, the bigger the accusation. I didn't even know such an economy existed at the time. I was just a twenty-six-year-old technocrat.

My age and gender were a big part of why people dismissed me. I was viewed as merely a sexual object. Sadness and anger overcame me. I could not understand why I deserved to have my character assassinated. To keep motivated, I had to remind myself of the big picture: every small success I, and women like me, achieved set a milestone for other women, who would have an easier time establishing themselves and raising their voices.

My family had already been skeptical about my career choice, but their fears were confirmed when I was smeared in the media. I was under so much pressure that I was hospitalized for stress-related health issues. But I did not want the situation to negatively affect my performance, so I decided to return to work after two weeks of sick leave.

Still, I continued to suffer a great deal emotionally because my family withdrew their support for what I was doing. They had supported me in my education under Taliban rule, and I was sure they would support me in my professional career, but they did not. It was the first time I had lost their approval. My parents had repeatedly warned me that I would have a hard time being accepted and respected in the security sector. And they were right.

Rather than back down, I became determined to prove that I was more than an object and that I was not doomed to serve men and bear their children, as the mentality of most conservative men in Afghanistan still dictates. In the years that followed, I was blamed for so many incidents. Explosions, the murders of journalists, even child abuse—they were all somehow my fault. To add to the stress of what was circulating in the media and online, my mother, a respected gynecologist, also started to feel disrespected and humiliated. She had always been proud of her profession and felt that she made an important contribution to society through her work. At that time, her pride was diminished because people kept making embarrassing accusations about my family, and it broke her heart.

I was able to bear all of the humiliation and personal attacks, but my family's pain was almost unbearable. Now my parents are still in Kabul, and we are looking for ways to get them out. Neither of them can work because they are in hiding. The Taliban will not forget their connection to me, so they keep changing their location. My family is also in danger because they are educated, because of their activities in different organizations, and because of the direct way they have criticized Taliban violence.

Through my work, I have always wanted to encourage women to be brave and assert their will. In the ministry, I found both female and male allies who helped me to get more involved, and that's how I was able to achieve some of my goals. Under the current circumstances, everything has changed dramatically.

The Taliban is out to destroy everything we have built. But the views of Afghans in the country have changed. It will be up to the younger generation to reflect upon and understand what is causing tensions. The coming months, or maybe even years, will be tough. Life in general, from going to the health centre to returning to a job to having a functioning legal system, will be very difficult. Yet I believe there are ways to preserve the gains we have made, by creating platforms for decision-making.

We need to allow diverse voices to speak out along-side the Taliban. As long as compromises can be reached

with the Taliban, there will be bright spots that will hope-
fully lead to a bipartisan government.

There are two reasons why the Taliban might be willing to listen and compromise. First, it needs international
legitimacy to govern. The Taliban used to be an insurgent
group that we called a terrorist group because it behaved
like a terrorist group. But now it is behaving diplomati-
cally, or at least wants to appear to be diplomatic in order
to be accepted as a legitimate government. Only international legitimacy could ward off interference from other,
powerful countries.

Second, the Taliban needs financial support. Legiti-
mizing a country on the international stage is not cheap.
Oppressing your own citizens, on the other hand, is cheap
because it only requires you to feed yourself. However,
Afghanistan is not a quiet country and its citizens will not
easily accept oppression. We have been a noisy nation
for the last twenty years. We have learned how to make
our voices heard. In a country where nearly 70 percent of
the population is twenty-four or younger, there is a strong
desire for progress. Keeping a loud and demanding young
population in check takes a lot of money and patience,
which the Taliban doesn't have.

I left two months before the collapse and joined the
National Defense University in Washington, D.C., for a
program designed to build U.S. partners' capacity for

countering terrorism and irregular warfare. The plan was to return to Afghanistan and join the security sector again.

To be honest, I haven't developed a concrete plan for where to go from here, because I'm still reeling from current events in Afghanistan and I've been busy taking care of the people who are still there. I have been thinking about how much it would hurt me to be labelled an exile one day. No matter where I am, though, I feel a strong connection to my country. Right now, I am focused on my studies so that one day I can return to Afghanistan with another master's degree, and I can serve my country with the added benefit of my new skills and knowledge.

Even if I had the opportunity to build a career outside of Afghanistan, I would not turn my back on my country. Not even if our colourful flag remains replaced by the black-and-white flag of the Taliban. I would want to be part of the new order, because I strongly believe in making positive changes from within. I will always try to find ways within this system to continue fighting for women's rights.

MINA SHARIF

Mina Sharif was born in Kabul during the Soviet occupation. In 1984, she and her family were granted asylum in Canada, where she grew up. In early 2005, she returned to Afghanistan as a volunteer radio instructor. She stayed until 2019, working for various media campaigns with a focus on educational content for children. She cofounded the Sisters 4 Sisters mentoring program for socially marginalized children in Afghanistan, and she was the executive producer for the second and third seasons of *Baghch-e-Simsim*, the Afghan version of *Sesame Street*. She was also the director of a television and radio series called *Voice of Afghan Youth*, hosted by Afghan children throughout the country. In her current role, Sharif works with numerous relief efforts for Afghanistan from her base in Canada.

I WAS BORN in Kabul at a time of unrest and uncertainty, in the early years of the Soviet occupation. My father was a news anchor and my mother taught literature. Many families chose to remain in Afghanistan, and that was the

plan for us as well, until overnight it became a matter of life and death. My parents fled with me, their one-year-old child, without a chance to say goodbye to their siblings or parents. As tragic as it must have been to lose their home, professions, and country, the hardest part was leaving without a goodbye. When my mother was reunited with her father decades later, she sobbed as she hugged him at the airport, and I understood that the severed human connections were the hardest of all the challenges.

The experience of fleeing Afghanistan was a traumatic one that went on for years before we landed in Canada and made a claim for asylum, when I was four. Though I did experience the escape with my parents, to me it was always their story. I don't have clear memories of life in Afghanistan or our time living as refugees before we arrived in Canada, but in some way my body always sensed it as a trauma that I shouldn't ask about too much. Eventually, I became an Afghan refugee all over again as an adult. Now there is no need for me to ask what suddenly losing so much feels like. I have my own memories of it.

Growing up in Canada, I was close with my immediate and extended family, who had found their way to each other in the Toronto area. Like many Afghans, I have a lot of cousins, and they provided a built-in circle of friends for me as a child. We were exposed to Afghan culture in a way that was so normalized, I found myself surprised a few times when visiting the homes of non-Afghans. I remember being about seven and wondering why there were no deep-red embroidered rugs at my classmate's house. I didn't think homes looked right without them.

Our weekends were full of life as my parents and their siblings sang Afghan songs and played instruments like the harmonia, tabla, and tambourine. We, the cousins, rented movies and lip-synced to Western pop songs, interrupted only when our mothers called us to eat from the elaborate spreads of baked rice infused with carrots and raisins, sides of spinach and chicken curry, and my favourite finely chopped salad of tomatoes, cucumber, and onions with mint and lots of lemon. We camped in the summers and cooked eggs with tomatoes over fires. This felt like enough connection to my culture for a long time.

When I was twenty-three, Afghanistan discovered me in Canada. I was offered a volunteer opportunity to support mostly women-managed radio stations across five provinces there. It had not occurred to me that my interest in radio would ever afford me the chance to work in the country of my birth. I hesitated to go, even when they offered me the position, because I thought six months sounded long. To everyone's surprise, I was on a plane to Kabul in February 2005. If you had asked me a few months prior, I would have told you I didn't expect to see Afghanistan in my lifetime. I hadn't even considered it as an option. In the end, I wound up staying in Afghanistan for nearly fifteen years.

I was in love before the plane hit the tarmac, and I can conjure that rush of emotion even now. There's specific magic in landing as a returnee that only a displaced diaspora can understand. Being raised away from my homeland meant that my first visit to Afghanistan was a reunion with a place I had no memory of. I loved everything from the first minute of my arrival, including the chaos of the airport, with people yelling and screaming in languages that were mine.

As excited as I was, I admittedly struggled to get my bearings when it came to work and daily life in Afghanistan. I wanted to be as useful as possible at work, and I wanted to be liked. I couldn't tell if I was more Afghan or more foreign, and in almost every interaction I had to decide or someone else would decide for me. My Afghan face often caused foreigners to assume I was willing and happy to translate their needs. My passport and decision to move to Afghanistan often caused Afghans to assume I was arrogant and rich. The challenges associated with being a part of the diaspora took some time to manoeuvre around, and I experienced many enlightening moments throughout my time in Afghanistan.

I remember my first work-related trip outside of Kabul, to Logar, which was less than two hours away. My three Canadian colleagues and I were led to a mountain-top where a radio station called Milli Paigham broadcast. The driver stopped the car where the road ended and told us that the station was high up on the mountain in order to ensure the best reception, so we would have to hike the rest of the way. As we made our way up the snowy mountain, our driver, who was leading the way, asked us to step into the footprints he left in the snow, so we would know each step we took was safe from mines.

After a steep walk up to an altitude that left us a little breathless, we made it to the radio station. My three colleagues and I met the station manager, a thin man with a beard and an Afghan Pakol hat. We were there to introduce ourselves and talk about equipment his station might need. We were truly excited, eager to dive into our jobs. Instead, the station manager interrogated me. He wanted to know why, as an Afghan woman, I was there alone without my family. He didn't look at me when he spoke, and he completely ignored the foreigners I was with, merely nodding in their direction when he referred to them as "kafirs," which means infidels. It was so stressful for me. I didn't yet know how to change the conversation back to business. So I answered his questions, telling him yes, my father was entirely on board with my travelling alone. I explained that the people I was with were my colleagues. That no, I had no relationship to the driver (who was politely waiting outside the meeting room). Meanwhile, my colleagues thought this was an Afghan bonding moment and quietly smiled the entire time. Later, when they asked what *kafir* meant, because they had noticed he said it in their direction, I said it meant foreigner. In later years, all my foreign colleagues learned the word, as did Afghan returnees.

Two years later, in 2007, I saw that station manager again. This time, I was working in the private sector, and we were creating a network for provincially based radio stations. I met women such as Zakia Zaki, a station manager in Jabal Seraj who was later assassinated. I met station managers from all around the country, some as young as twenty years old. I enjoyed conversations with them about where they had travelled from, and so many of them warmly invited me to visit their home province as their guest. Then I saw the station manager from Logar. I was nervous, worried that I was about to be scolded. He spoke to me, nodding along to his own words. He said their radio station had just started a youth program and it was really popular and that we should share a recording of it with the other stations so they could do the same. He didn't make direct eye contact, but I was used to that by now, understanding that most men just did not do that with women. My nerves relaxed and I couldn't resist telling him that we had met before.

"Yes, I know. You came to the station."

And that was it. He told me how much further the station's reach was now, and our team should come and see.

I've thought about that incident for years. Some might hear it and think the man had been enlightened, or that he now respects women and has had second thoughts about his earlier behaviour. That's not what I saw. As I reflected on the first meeting we had at the radio station, I realized he had likely been caught off guard to see an Afghan woman when he'd expected foreigners. I wouldn't say this is true about every man I encountered in Afghanistan, but I think that particular man was more surprised than offended to see me there—an Afghan woman in a position of importance, with whom he had to negotiate. And what if he was not surprised but appalled by my presence? That was okay too. Because in 2007, at least professionally, his personal feelings could not take centre stage. By that time, the social environment that had been fostered meant that he had no choice but to deal with me if he wanted to succeed. I truly don't care if he liked that he had to work with me or only tolerated it. My experience was a far more pleasant one either way.

The rapid increase in opportunities for young Afghans from the year 2001 to 2021, particularly for women, made it feel like everyone had begun to participate in the new liberties being offered by a greater sense of security. Whether it was office work, advocacy, or even families picnicking and enjoying the outdoors together, I saw changes in every province I went to, and consistently more and more as time went on.

I hear dismissals of what I saw as the experiences of a privileged few. What an easy blanket statement to make. It is true that the funds, approximately three trillion U.S. dollars spent in Afghanistan over the last two decades, were spent poorly and often in ways that appeared to fill the pockets of corrupt Afghan leaders or the donors themselves. However, in my opinion, the many corruptions around aid money are not the defining feature of the past twenty years. Instead, I believe a collective sense of security and safety is what moved Afghanistan in a positive direction. Within community parameters for religious, family, tribal, or ethnic life, there was a sense of freedom that emerged from much of the country's being safer than it had been for decades.

The effects of this increased sense of trust and freedom were not just felt by a few elites in Kabul, and the suggestion that only a small urban centre had been modernized while the majority in the provinces remained Taliban supporters is false. While Afghanistan was never fully liberated from the Taliban, and therefore never fully secure, much of the country felt safe enough to have girls in school and work in support of Afghan society. The people I met did not miss the grim days of the Taliban, not even in the most rural of areas. It's true that the provincial villages received very few of the benefits from the donor money, if any at all, as most funds were spent in the cities. Although those areas remained isolated and ignored, that does not equate to preference for Taliban rule. Much of Afghanistan is conservative, yes. But in areas that felt safe from the Taliban, Afghans led their lives the way they saw fit—within their own parameters that were in line with Afghan culture, not Taliban ideology. Where there was conservative Islam, there was also Afghan music, Afghan art, family picnics, and poetry. Such freedom to live as Afghans has always been important and is not in line with the claim of majority support for the Taliban outside of cities.

Appreciation for Afghan art, culture, and poetry has always existed in every province. While filming in Ghor province, a remote area barely touched by aid, our team was given a tour of a sculpture garden. In a village hours away from any city, women invited me to dance with them to songs playing on a cellphone that was charging on a generator. There was art, theatre, expression, music, laughter, colourful clothing, and education—all of it Afghan. Had the allied forces defeated the Taliban, as they'd promised was their goal during the twenty years of occupying Afghanistan, I believe this is what much of Afghanistan would look like today. Thousands of years of rich history were created by the majority. The implication that Taliban ideology was lurking in all those hearts is dreadfully inaccurate.

—

Today I am back in Canada. I returned in 2019, intending to go back to Kabul six weeks later. For personal reasons, I had to give up that ticket and stay. I planned to go back as soon as possible. I still have that ticket in my email, and all my personal possessions are being stored in the basement of a friend's home in Kabul: my Afghan embroidered dresses, the photos I had hung on my walls, and even my diaries are waiting for me. The plan was to reunite with my home and my things. Instead, my books, tapestries, and treasured gemstone necklace will likely be looted or destroyed by a foot soldier of an insurgency that would surely target me for being a believer in Afghan culture, a believer in the capacity of Afghan women to lead as they have throughout our history, and a defender of the Afghan flag that it stands against.

Now I spend my time advocating and using my voice however I can to prevent silence around Afghan issues. That means sharing my experiences with the diaspora, so they understand the beauty of where they come from, without depending on misleading headlines. It means speaking up on social media outlets to highlight the many contradictions of this unwelcome occupation of my country.

The question of what happens to my people now feels like a block of cement in my chest. The hunger, the collapse of the economy, and the brutality that we are already seeing are all crises. Add drought and illness. Add targeted killings. Add genocide. These are all either happening or at high risk of happening, because they align with what the Taliban has done in the past and is on course to do again.

But what really plagues me—a question that headlines often aren't interested in considering—is what happens to the soul of my people. What about those women with whom I danced? What about the children who learned to play classical Afghan musical instruments? What about the women who once managed massive groups of people, now confined to their homes, who are unlikely to prosper in any professional way? And most of all, what about their trust in the world?

I don't believe in reinstating a heavy international presence under the guise of rebuilding Afghanistan. What the world did was try to show Afghans how to live. That was not necessary and never had been. Westerners, myself included in the early years, thought we were showing Afghanistan democracy. We thought we were bringing Afghanistan ideas on how to include women as leaders in society. This is nonsense that we believed was necessary because we only had a view from outside. But Afghans have had women in leadership throughout history. Afghans simply needed to trust that the space was safe, not to be told how to live. And they can only trust the space if it is their own. The Afghan people, without inter-ference, must elect an Afghan government.

The world must learn the difference between sup-port and interference. Support means monetary aid, yes, because this is not a mess we got into alone. Without interference, an elected Afghan government would likely be far more conservative than what someone like me is accustomed to in Canada. But we don't need to recreate what life is like in the West. We need Afghans to decide what is best for their own country. And I assure you, our history assures you, that what they want is not what is happening now. Afghans want nothing more than to live peaceful, healthy lives surrounded by their own beauti-ful culture. Then, much like that hospitable radio station manager I met in 2007, they will smile and welcome you all to visit as their guests.

RADA AKBAR

Born in 1988, Rada Akbar is an activist and artist who uses her art to speak out against misogyny and oppression. Her work consists of a mixture of wearable monuments, performance, painting, photography, curation, and installation pieces. It has been displayed in numerous national and international exhibitions. In 2015, she received an honourable mention from the UNICEF Photo of the Year Award. In 2020, her art exhibit *Abarzanan—Superwomen*, which celebrates pioneering Afghan women, was featured in the *New York Times*. In 2021, she received the Prince Claus Seed Award, which recognizes emerging artists and cultural practitioners.

IN OCTOBER 2018, I was preparing for the launch of a project called *Peace Runway* in Lahore, Pakistan. The project was to be a fashion show. It was conceived in a conversation between journalists, civil society members, and entrepreneurs, and it was funded by the U.S. government in an effort to strengthen the relationship between

Afghanistan and Pakistan. The aim of the show was to bring the fashion of the two countries together in a celebration of local craft and culture. I was just a hobby fashion designer at the time, but I was asked to direct the part of the exhibit that focused on Afghan fashion.

Weeks before the show, my Kabul flat was robbed. The only items stolen were my computer, its charger, and eight hard drives. Jewellery, cameras, an iPad, and other valuables, including some cash, were still there. But the entire archive of my work from over a decade was gone. Several projects that were in the making, scripts for upcoming performance pieces, and my photography archives were all on those drives.

I quickly enlisted the police, the interior ministry, and even my sister Shaharzad, who was an adviser to the president at that time, to find my most precious possessions. Many people who knew my work, including some ambassadors and their wives, did their part to try to find the missing drives. They even tapped into their networks of military intelligence to help track down the robber. Sleepless nights, anxious days, and panic attacks followed as I searched for my life's work. Why? I kept asking, without ever finding an answer. In the end, I wound up empty-handed, and I was devastated.

The confluence of the robbery with the fashion show held in Pakistan, which I decided to participate in despite the trauma I had experienced just weeks earlier, all inspired me to create my next series of art exhibitions, which I called

Abarzanan—Superwomen. My idea was to bring together Afghanistan's past, present, and future; showcase Afghan traditions and culture; and honour my country's most inspiring women. I was in my element once again, and the project quickly became the centre of my world—and also my saviour—as I started to build my body of work back up from nothing.

I began by selecting eight inspiring women—four historical figures and four contemporary women—to feature. Gawharshad Begum (1378–1457), an empress of the Timurid dynasty, became the anchor of the whole project. Married to Emperor Shahrukh Timurid (1377–1447), she moved the capital of the dynasty from Samarqand to Herat, and she led a cultural renaissance that elevated Persian language and culture by patronizing many artists, philosophers, architects, musicians, and poets. She was also integral to changing the empire's architecture. The world-renowned Gawhar Shad Mosque in present-day Iran and Gawhar Shad Madrasa and Mausoleum in Herat are two of the many historical sites built under her guidance and vision. Gawharshad was also a skilled politician. Despite her wisdom and experience, she was blocked from ruling directly after her husband died. Instead of allowing the opportunity to take power pass her by, Gawharshad installed her favourite grandson as a puppet king and ruled the kingdom for more than ten years. Now, centuries later, she lives on as a symbol of women's power in the region.

Gawharshad seemed like the right person around whom to orient the series, because she demonstrated the powerful contribution women are capable of making to Afghan culture, even when they are not given permission to do so. I wanted the subjects featured in the exhibition to inspire women to step up and realize their full potential today. As the idea evolved during its first year, I added women of other nationalities to show that regardless of what time or place we come from, we are all fighting the same fight. Women have been denied power and erased from the history books all over the world.

In collaboration with Afghan and international artists, we created wearable artworks, paintings, and installations to honour each subject's contribution to history. I wanted each piece to carry a story of Afghan heritage and female strength to bring my vision of an empowered future to life. We honoured the past by showcasing Afghan traditions and culture, including embroidery, tile patterns, and design, as well as traditional jewellery and metalwork.

The makers of the wearable artworks each practised a traditional Afghan trade that is at risk of being lost. The embroidery patterns used in Gawharshad Begum's piece, a modern dress, were inspired by the patterns that appear on her tomb and in the exquisite artistry she commissioned on buildings such as the Gawhar Shad Mosque and the Gawhar Shad Madrasa and Mausoleum. Similar traditional patterns and techniques were used across all of the pieces in the exhibit, as was Nasta'līq, the predominant style of Persian calligraphy, which was also developed under the reign of Gawharshad Begum.

The first *Abarzanan* exhibition opened on March 8, 2019. Three of the women inspiring the collection were under twenty-five years old, emphasizing the extraordinary strength and determination that Afghan girls and women exhibit each day. It was the beginning of a series of *Abarzanan* exhibitions that celebrated Afghan and international superwomen. The second and third versions of the exhibition came to life in the two years that followed. We celebrated another eight women each time, bringing in women from Iran, Pakistan, and even Honduras as well. The exhibitions were a resounding success. They provoked many conversations on women's rights in Afghanistan, have been viewed by thousands of people, and were covered by national and international media.

And thus we brought together Afghanistan's past and its future, its rulers and artists, and its new and old traditions to usher in a new era of peacebuilding and reconciliation. My end goal was to use the exhibitions to establish a women's history museum in Afghanistan. I even secured a space for the museum in Kabul's Darul Aman Palace after negotiating with the government, a plan that unfortunately will not come to fruition under the Taliban regime.

—

When I was approached to submit some words for this book, the pieces of writing that appear below immediately came to mind. The first three pieces were shared at the openings of the first three *Abarzanan* exhibitions in Kabul. The final piece is a speech I gave to a European Union panel after Kabul fell.

I thought it would be interesting to present these texts together, dated like a diary. Here you will see how the project grew from its first to its third exhibition, and how I adapted it to the changing political situation in Afghanistan over those years. You will see changes in my creative process that respond to changes in the security and stability of Afghanistan—in particular a rise in targeting of and violence against women. For example, in the 2021 exhibit, we chose to feature eight women, both well-known and ordinary women, who had left a legacy after losing their lives. Sadly, many women who walked the streets of Afghanistan in the last decades were killed as a result of their free-spirited activities and human rights activism. I often ask myself, What contributions could they have made if their lives had been spared?

KABUL, MARCH 8, 2019

There seems to be a global misunderstanding that Afghan women are victims and need saving, or that we are not capable of defining our own priorities. The women featured in my exhibitions, and the Afghan women you see every day around you, are proof that these assumptions couldn't be farther from the truth.

As you'll notice in the biographies of the women featured in this exhibition—such as Rabia Balkhi, the tenth-century poet; Her Majesty Queen Soraya Tarzi, 1899–1968; Kubra Noorzai, 1932–1986, the first woman minister of Afghanistan; or the vibrant young Negin Khpalwak, the first female conductor and leader of the all-female Zohra Orchestra of Afghanistan—women have been fighting for our rights for centuries. Yes, at times, we have had to take a step back because of the decisions of global powers or the powerful men and groups within our communities, but we've never been silent. The world simply wasn't listening. That will not be the case anymore.

While today we celebrate abarzanan, superwomen, I know that in every home in Afghanistan there lives an abarzan, a superwoman.

Every woman who fights for the right of her children to go to school is a superwoman, as is every girl who dares to go to school or choose her own attire. So too is every one of my sisters who continue to work and earn their own income despite harassment and violence from the Taliban, and every woman who quietly saves money so that someday she can file for divorce and leave an abusive marriage. Every mother who secretly takes birth control so she has control over her own body is a superwoman, and so is every woman who appears to have given up and given in to violence and abuse but writes and thinks about freedom. No matter which corner of this heartbroken country she lives in, to me, every Afghan woman is a superwoman.

I'm honoured to feature some of the abarzanan, the brave women of my country, in this exhibit. I am grateful to them for inspiring me with their resilience, courage, and small acts of rebellion every day.

KABUL, MARCH 8, 2020

Welcome, and happy International Women's Day!

It feels unjust to celebrate this day while the basic human rights of women in Afghanistan face unprecedented threats. Even as we gather today to celebrate the strength of women, the contributions women have made to this country and to our shared world, I can't escape the rage that looms above my head.

We, Afghan women and our allies, are righteously enraged.

We are right to be angry about Donald Trump bargaining away what few rights we have gained by endangering our lives.

We are right to be angry about our sisters and brothers who put themselves on the front lines to defend our rights and freedoms, only to be repaid by international politicians shaking hands at places we were barred from.

We are right to be angry on behalf of the teachers, students, vaccinators, activists, and journalists who braved threats of rape and violence to move this country forward, only to be met with global indifference.

We are righteously enraged at the silent disregard of our voices and stories.

This righteous rage did not just appear from nowhere. It emerged from centuries of women's voices being silenced and their needs being put at the bottom of the to-do list. It comes from the blood of Malalai Kakar, from the stones hurled at Rukhshana, a nineteen-year-old woman from Ghor who was kidnapped and stoned to death in October 2015 by the Taliban. It comes from media coverage of political men smirking as we drown in our own blood. It comes from generations of powerful men telling us to wait. Wait for the right to go to school. For the right to be seen as a human being. For the right to custody of the children we birthed. For the right to hold positions of power. For our turn.

This exhibition is a response to those powerful men. They want us to remain within the boundaries they negotiated for us. They want us to be silent, obedient, fearful. We will not be. If there's anything we can learn from the history of women's struggles in Afghanistan and in the region, it is that even the most oppressive regimes were not able to poison the seeds of rebellion and freedom that grow in our hearts. We'll not go back. We will not submit to the boundaries others create for us. We will not be silent.

Now is our time. Now is our turn.

We will teach our daughters about Khalida Popalzai and her dream for every girl to play sports freely and without fear. We will teach our sons about the feminist and rebellious Forugh Farrokhzad's poetry, about loving without confinement. We will teach our children about Asma Jahangir, the human rights defender, about fighting for freedom even if you are imprisoned. We will teach our children about Rukhshana, who preferred death to slavery. We will honour these women and their dreams by continuing our fight for a better world, a world where no girl feels less than and no woman is prohibited from being her true self, her most free self.

It's a duty to tell these stories when the world refuses to listen. *Abarzanan*'s goal is to celebrate centuries of strong and influential role models. We came into existence to change the current narrative that identifies the women of this country as victims. And we're here to say that Afghan women are not victims but champions. We have been fighting to make ourselves heard throughout history, even when the most powerful forces drown out our voices with bombs. And we'll continue this fight with every new day.

We will not accept the bare minimum. We will fight for the right to work and the right to love. We will fight for the right to education and to be in positions of power. We will fight for the right to speak our minds and the right to control our own bodies. We are not less than and we do not deserve fewer rights than anyone. We'll not adhere to a racist standard that says we should be okay with just the basics because we are from Afghanistan. The mission is not over when bombs stop going off in our neighbourhoods. We deserve more than schools for girls, more than the right to work for women who dress or live a certain way. We want equal rights for every single person, and we'll fight for those rights even as we are betrayed by those who once patted themselves on the back for "saving" us.

Thank you all for being here today. By being here, you are a part of this mission. Please help us spread the word about this exhibition and the brave women featured here. Help us water the seeds of freedom and justice.

—

KABUL, MARCH 8, 2021

Dear lost treasures, I feel deeply saddened to be here today. It feels devastating to deliver these words. The empty space in the room is burning my soul and heart. When we started *Abarzanan* three years ago, I never imagined we would be holding an exhibition for the deceased. But in the absence of justice and peace, we know the things we once thought were impossible become our reality. Today, we celebrate and honour another eight superwomen, who have all been killed for their beliefs and activities. All of these women fought for a better and brighter future. And they all lost their lives while fighting to protect women, children, art, and nature.

It's hard not to think of these women as we are losing both well-known and unrecognized champions like them every day in Afghanistan. We are living through some of the darkest moments as we watch the daily loss of life of journalists, writers, activists, human rights defenders, mothers, fathers, children. The world no longer seems to be shaken as our bodies collapse, one after the other. Justice seems unattainable, as our stories are denied by the same people who came here to fight terrorism and claimed they'd do right by Afghan women.

I've been told that the world is tired of us, tired of Afghanistan and its bloodshed. Can the world imagine how tired we are? Does the world know how helpless we feel when decisions about our future, about our lives— and our youth—are made in Doha and Washington? Do they know that we walk on seas of blood every day? Do they know the scars we have in our hearts and souls? Do they know that death is breathing down our necks? This may sound like a horror movie, but does anyone care?

To the eight women we honour through this exhibition today and to the victims of terrorist attacks, our lost lights, I wish I could tell you we are living better lives. I wish I could say we never lost any of you. I hope you are resting in peace. Because we are not living in peace. It is an honour to be here. To speak to you. To be able to tell parts of your stories. To remember you.

PARIS, JANUARY 8, 2022

On March 8, 2021, I stood in an empty hall in Kabul to launch my exhibition titled *Abarzanan—Superwomen*. The exhibition remembered and celebrated women human rights defenders, artists, and activists killed for their work. The security situation in Kabul was so tumultuous at the time that I couldn't risk opening my exhibition to the public. I didn't want people to die in a terrorist attack while looking at my art. So, unlike in previous years, it was an invitation-only event. Having lived in Kabul for most of my life, I couldn't imagine that things could get worse, and yet they have.

Today, Afghan women are barred from virtually all aspects of public life. Girls are still prohibited from attending secondary schools in the country. Kabul University, a hub for art and activism, has been closed to women since the takeover in August 2021. Women who are teachers,

journalists, artists, activists, lawyers, and judges are confined to their homes and living in fear as the Taliban hunt
them down. The lucky few, like me, have been able to
make it out of the country through evacuation flights or
by road. Many of us are now refugees.

The journey has been long and tough. I was lucky to
save my life, but I left behind my home, my loved ones,
my dreams and aspirations, my identity, and a piece of my
heart and soul. So did many others. My current status is
official refugee, with an uncertain future in Paris, where I
now live. It is a difficult transition to start everything again
from zero. I must re-establish my career and life here and
rediscover my voice and identity in this new context.

I never wanted to leave my country and never imagined I would be forced to. For years, I've advocated for
human rights using the tools I have: my camera, my
paintbrush, and my voice. Under the Taliban, I knew that
would no longer be possible. Now I turn on the news to
see my fellow countrywomen being whipped, beaten, and
detained by the Taliban for requesting the most basic of
rights: education for all Afghan citizens.

Since the Taliban occupied the country on August 15,
2021, reports show that they have killed musicians, a com-
edian, activists, and countless other civilians. They've
forcibly displaced Hazaras, an ethnic and religious minority
that has faced centuries-long oppression and discrimination in Afghanistan, taken their homes and lands, and

terrorized their children. They've published new guide-
lines for the press, barring them from reporting that may
"have a negative impact on the public's attitude." These
are arbitrary rules used to legitimize the detainment and
torture of journalists and the closure of independent media
outlets. They've beaten up women on the streets for being
outside the house without a companion or for dressing in
ways the Taliban doesn't approve of. They've killed the
teenage son of a police officer because of his father's work,
according to local media sources. The list of their atrocities
is endless. And these are only the atrocities we hear about,
the ones that are happening in big cities with media presence. What Taliban members in rural areas of the country
do—without any oversight—is a darkness we may never
hear about.

For years, the people of Afghanistan tolerated indig-
nity and war because we were able to send our children to
school. Every Afghan family knows the importance of education. We've risked our lives in order to protect this right.
Teachers have been killed. Students have been poisoned.
Schools have been burned. And yet our daughters showed
up at school the next day. Until the Taliban took over.

I am astounded and broken by the silence of the world
in the face of so many denials of basic human rights
by the Taliban. It smacks of a particular kind of racism
that accepts lower standards for certain people. It gives
the world permission to tell us to be content with only

the right to live, while we continue to live under the threat of violence and brutality and beg for basic rights.

Afghanistan is now the only country in the world where girls are denied the right to education. Education shouldn't be available only for those who comply with Taliban dress codes. The millions of women and girls left behind are losing their hope and faith as they begin to see the ways the world has forgotten about them. We cannot and should not forget about them. We must work collectively to protect their full human rights. Afghan women and girls don't deserve fewer rights just because they are in Afghanistan. They should be able to make their own decisions about their own lives.

And if we give in to the false propaganda that Afghan people—the same people who sent millions of women to work and girls to schools—agree with the Taliban's way of doing things, we are complicit in their abuse. Now is the time to make it clear that we stand with Afghan women as they fight back and share their dream to build a safer, more equal world. Whether it is in the streets of Paris or of Kabul, Afghan women are saying no to the Taliban and its vision. Is the world courageous enough to listen to us?

I believe one woman's liberation is tied to all women's liberation. We can't breathe freely in Paris if our sisters are chained in Kabul. Fundamentalism, extremism, and misogyny are one monster with many faces, and feeding the monster in one part of the world strengthens it in others. Afghan women are not less than anyone and we deserve our full human rights. We deserve freedom and dignity. We deserve to fulfill our dreams.

In this dark and difficult moment, Afghan women don't need saviours. We need sisterhood and solidarity. Afghan women are brave and resilient. Our sisters in Afghanistan have been marching in different parts of the country for their rights as the Taliban brutally beats and tear-gases them. We want the world to stand with us and support us. We want the world to march with us.

For you, solidarity might look like asking your government to refuse to recognize the Taliban as a legitimate government. You might demand that it closely monitor the Taliban's actions on the ground and ensure they do not target women, ethnic and religious minorities, the free press, journalists, or artists. Solidarity might look like asking your government to continue to provide support to local media outlets in Afghanistan so Afghans can continue to access a free press.

For those UN special representatives who are no longer in the country, solidarity would look like putting in requests to visit the country and launch fact-finding missions about the Taliban's atrocities. It would look like increasing the UN's international humanitarian staff on the ground to correct the disappointing way they handled the U.S. withdrawal.

So much about the future of my country is unclear. One thing, however, is very clear. The Taliban has reversed and will continue to reverse human rights gains in Afghanistan. Whether it's through restrictions on the free press or on women's involvement in public, political, social, and cultural life, or through bringing back cutting off hands and public hangings, the Taliban has already taken my homeland back a century. The final nail in the coffin of human rights and freedom in Afghanistan will be to legitimize this terrorist organization as a government. It will make the international community complicit in the Taliban's atrocities and abuse of power.

One day, I hope I will be able to return to my homeland and breathe in the sweet scent of the jojoba trees in our courtyard, to drink green tea with friends at a café downtown, to engage in hours-long conversations with fellow artists over a meal enjoyed under the Afghan sky. I don't know if that day will ever come. But I know it will not be possible if the world ignores the Taliban and its atrocities and forgets about the people of Afghanistan, a people yearning for freedom.

CONCLUSION
BY NAHID SHAHALIMI

ACROSS HISTORY, WOMEN have faced discrimination and experienced limitations simply because of their gender. When women had no ability to form laws in the absence of voting rights, they were forced to comply with rules set by the men in power. In marriage, there was a time when women did not have the right to own property, and wives were legally under the control of their husbands. At times, they were beaten or imprisoned with impunity. In some countries, women are still beaten in the streets.

It is because of the many bold activists and ordinary women who took a stand that we no longer face the same degree of oppression by unjust systems today. Without them, my life—all of our lives—would be radically different, from the clothes I wear to the words I write in the pages of this book, to the decisions I make about my body, to the values I instill in my own daughters. Underlying the choices we take for granted, as if they were given to us by nature, are fundamental rights that many women and girls around the world only have access to if they are willing to put their lives at risk.

It seems we have come a long way. But have we, really? Have we cleared a path for all girls to follow? Have we ensured that fundamental rights and freedoms are being upheld for all women around the world?

On August 15th, 2021, amid a spectacle that filled the front pages of every newspaper, Afghan women and girls lost many of their basic human rights overnight when Kabul fell into the hands of the Taliban. Just a few weeks later, the media moved on and the world averted its eyes as international fatigue kicked in.

Many of those women are still in Afghanistan today. Women protesters go head to head with Taliban foot soldiers and find themselves looking straight down the barrels of machine guns as they scream tirelessly for "Jobs! Food! Freedom!" Many have been whipped, pushed, pepper-sprayed, and arrested for raising their voices. Some have even been abducted in the middle of the night after returning to their homes.

In January 2022, independent United Nations human rights experts issued an official warning on the UN website saying that "Taliban leaders in Afghanistan are institutionalizing large-scale and systemic gender-based discrimination and violence against women and girls." We are at a crucial juncture, not just in the history of Afghanistan and the region, but also when it comes to the achievements of women around the world.

The words of the women in this book are the strongest evidence of that claim. When the hard-won rights of Afghans are used as bargaining chips for political deals behind closed doors, it sends a signal that women's rights and human rights are negotiable. As long as rights can be taken from Afghan women, so too can they be rolled back with the stroke of a pen in countries like the United States. If we are to continue to make real progress, women's rights must be the undisputable standard for everyone—including the Taliban—to uphold.

Now, more than ever, we as women and global citizens need to join forces and demand gender equality. We cannot stand by and wait another 135 years for the global gender gap to close. According to the World Economic Forum's 2021 report, that's how long it will take at the rate we are going.

Movements built around hashtags like #insolidarity are important, but what we need is true global solidarity that goes beyond keyboard activism. In order to raise the voices of courageous Afghan women from the streets of Afghanistan, we need experts like the Afghan women featured in this book, and we need to give them platforms to speak for themselves. We also need the global support of those in power, and especially women in power.

When Afghan women are able to launch campaigns, establish steering committees, form lobbying groups, and make recommendations to women's organizations, UN agencies, and governmental and nongovernmental agencies without impediment, they become a powerful force. With strong support, no draconian ideology that aims to suppress women's rights or human rights will hinder the pursuit of socio-political equality and economic justice.

For all those activists and ordinary women who have sacrificed their lives, and for the future generations of women and girls, we will continue to fight. We are still here, and we will continue to raise our voices. But we will see the change we need only when everyone—women, men, Afghans, and the international community—stands shoulder to shoulder in true solidarity.

AFTERWORD

THIS PROJECT WAS filled with challenges. Many of the essays in the book evolved from interviews, and any ambiguities were clarified in further conversations.

Some of the original conversations and texts were conducted or written in Dari or German, but most in English. We had to decide during the editing and translation processes how intensively we should intervene in the language and in the content of the essays. We decided to maintain individual tones and gave preference to each woman's voice over perfect grammar.

In order to ensure that no contributor was put in harm's way, we had to accept that some women were subjecting themselves to self-censorship.

We did not want to let too much time pass because of the urgency of the topic. I had less than two months to find the women who contributed to the book, conduct interviews, transcribe, translate, and proofread the essays. This English version was translated directly from the German version and re-edited in early January 2022.

To all of the women who contributed to this book and trusted me during a very vulnerable moment, I extend my deepest gratitude. We all see you.

ACKNOWLEDGEMENTS

FIRST, I WOULD like to thank my German publisher, Dr. Elisabeth Sandmann, without whose dedication, persistence, and faith in my work, none of the editions would have been possible. Particularly, I would like to thank the team of Elisabeth Sandmann Verlag, who worked tirelessly with me day and night and believed in the power of this book from the beginning. Lianna Adams deserves special acknowledgement for keeping the visual accompaniments to the book up-to-date.

I am deeply grateful to Margaret Atwood for writing an eloquent and heartfelt foreword that acknowledges the struggles women face around the world.

It was because of the support of the following individuals that the original German publication of this book was made possible. Some people's names we cannot mention for security reasons.

Kirsten Ackermann Piech, Myrtle Barrow, Marie Sophie von Bibra, Jan Stefan Findel and Susan Cummings Findel, Simona Fix, Bettina Fritsche Friedrich, Dr. Inge Haselsteiner, Cord Georg and Caroline Hasselmann,

Ulrike Beate Heidler, Hans Henning Ihlefeld, Brigitte Elisabeth Milse Dressel, Birgit Neiser, Eva Rapaport, Friedrich Karl Sandmann, Heike Schneeweiss, Jutta Speidel, Layla Waziri, Jermabelle Westner, Eva Römer, Florian Frohnholzer, Anne Stukenborg, Jan Russok, Homa Popal, Zohal Nelly Popal, Ila Yaqub, Hermine Kaiser, Philipp Sandmann, Mina Yaqub, Joyce Korotkin, Shakila Ibrahimkhail, Nina Yaqob, Geoff Blackwell, and Ruth Hobday.

As a final note, last but not least, I would like to thank Laura Dosky and the entire Penguin Canada team for believing in this project. They understood the value of each contributor and respected their vulnerability while allowing their voices and the tone of their language to shine through. Thank you for your ethical and professional way of working, and for making me feel welcome by giving me the freedom I needed to work.

REFERENCES

INTRODUCTION

Afghans make up one of the largest refugee populations worldwide "Afghanistan," UNHCR.

revered as a charismatic military leader and a deeply pious figure Ahmed Rashid, "The 100 Most Influential People of 2021: Abdul Ghani Baradar," *Time*, September 15, 2021.

ARYANA SAYEED

the Taliban has prevented girls from attending school after grade six Victor J. Blue and David Zucchino, "A Harsh New Reality for Afghan Women and Girls in Taliban-Run Schools," *New York Times*, September 20, 2021.

forced almost all women who worked for the previous government—and those who worked for private companies—to stay home "Kabul Government's Female Workers Told to Stay at Home by Taliban," *The Guardian*, September 19, 2021.

They have begun to ban music in parts of the country "Taliban Ban Music in Afghanistan's Eastern Province," *The New Arab*, February 1, 2022.

WASLAT HASRAT-NAZIMI

before the Taliban took power in 2021, about one thousand Afghan women were journalists "Fewer than 100 of Kabul's 700 Women Journalists Still Working," Reporters Without Borders, September 1, 2021.

about 47,000 innocent civilians have died Ellen Knickmeyer, "Cost of the Afghanistan War, in Lives and Dollars," AP News, August 17, 2021.

MARIAM SAFI

Seventeen years ago, hope replaced despair Mariam Safi, "UN Security Council Briefing on Afghanistan," NGO Working Group on Women, Peace, and Security, March 8, 2018.

In the first half of 2021, the United Nations Assistance Mission in Afghanistan (UNAMA) documented 5,183 civilian casualties "Afghanistan Protection of Civilians in Armed Conflict Midyear Update 2021," United Nations Assistance Mission in Afghanistan, July 26, 2021.

Comprising 46 percent of all civilian casualties, 32 percent were children and 14 percent were women Ibid.

HILA LIMAR

These simple letters cannot be read by 70.2 percent of women in Afghanistan "Literacy rate in Afghanistan increased to 43 per cent," interview by UNESCO, UNESCO Institute for Lifelong Learning, March 17, 2020.

consequences if 2.2 million girls—or 60 percent of all primary-school-aged children—cannot attend school "Education," UNICEF.

Each year of secondary schooling a young girl completes reduces her chance of early marriage "Educating Girls, Ending Child Marriage," World Bank, August 24, 2017.

a woman's earnings can increase by up to 20 percent for every additional year of schooling she completes as a girl Quentin T. Wodon, Claudio E. Montenegro, Hoa Nguyen, and Adenike Opeoluwa Onagoruwa, "Missed Opportunities: The High Cost of Not Educating Girls," The Cost of Not Educating Girls Series, Washington, D.C.: World Bank Group, July 11, 2018.

a child has died in Afghanistan every five hours over the past twenty years "One Child Killed or Maimed Every 5 Hours over 20 Years of War in Afghanistan," Save the Children, August 31, 2021.

Between 2001 and 2021, the school enrollment rate in Afghanistan has increased almost tenfold "The Right to Education: What's at Stake in Afghanistan? A 20-year Review," Paris: United Nations Educational, Scientific and Cultural Organization, 2021.

In half of the country's provinces, less than 20 percent of teachers are women "Afghanistan: Girls Struggle for an Education," Human Rights Watch, October 17, 2017.

Between 2017 and 2018, they tripled, and by the end of 2018, more than one thousand schools were closed because of constant armed conflict and the political situation in the country "Afghanistan Sees Three-fold Increase in Attacks on Schools in One Year," UNICEF, May 27, 2019.

RADA AKBAR

Today, Afghan women are barred from virtually all aspects of public life "UN: Taliban Attempting to Exclude Women, Girls from Public Life," *Al Jazeera*, January 17, 2022.

Girls are still prohibited from attending secondary schools in the country Emma Graham-Harrison, "Taliban Bans Girls from Secondary Education in Afghanistan," *The Guardian*, September 17, 2021.

They've forcibly displaced Hazaras Emma Graham-Harrison, "Taliban 'Forcibly Evicting' Hazaras and Opponents in Afghanistan," *The Guardian*, October 23, 2021.

have a negative impact on the public's attitude "Afghanistan: Taliban Severely Restrict Media," Human Rights Watch, October 1, 2021.

Afghanistan is now the only country in the world where girls are denied the right to education Tooba Neda Safi, "Afghanistan: The Only Country that Bans Girls' Education," *Geneva Solutions*, October 25, 2021.

CONCLUSION

Taliban leaders in Afghanistan are institutionalizing large-scale and systemic gender-based discrimination and violence "Afghanistan: Taliban Attempting to Steadily Erase Women and Girls from Public Life—UN Experts," United Nations Human Rights Office of the High Commissioner, January 17, 2022.

According to the World Economic Forum's 2021 report "Global Gender Gap Report 2021," World Economic Forum, March 2021.

PHOTO CREDITS

Photography on pages ii, viii, 52, 172, 180, and 182 by Nahid Shahalimi

Photography on page 6 by Dr. Isa Foltin

Photography on page 24 by Alena Sable

Photography on page 30 by Razia Barakzai

Photography on page 40 by Sherzaad Entertainment

Photography on page 60 by Fahim Farooq Photography

Photography on page 74 by David Fox

Photography on page 88 by Hosai Safi

Photography on page 98 by Ahmad Imani, courtesy of Roya Film House

Photography on page 104 by Wana Limar, courtesy of Visions for Children

Photography on page 118 by Shuhra Koofi

Photography on page 126 by Sabawoon Noori

Photography on page 136 by Mina Sharif

Photography on page 148 by Rada Akbar

CONTRIBUTORS' CREDITS

Foreword, pages 1–4 © 2022 Margaret Atwood

Introduction, pages 5, 7–23 © 2022 Nahid Shahalimi

Fereshteh Forough, pages 25–29 © 2022 Fereshteh
    Forough

Razia Barakzai, pages 31–39 © 2022 Razia Barakzai

Aryana Sayeed, pages 41–50 © 2022 Aryana Sayeed

Fatima Gailani, pages 51, 53–59 © 2022 Fatima Gailani

Waslat Hasrat-Nazimi, pages 61–72 © 2022 Waslat
    Hasrat-Nazimi

Manizha Wafeq, pages 73, 75–86 © 2022 Manizha Wafeq

Mariam Safi, pages 87, 89–96 © 2022 Mariam Safi

Roya Sadat, pages 97, 99–103 © 2022 Roya Sadat

Hila Limar, pages 105–117 © 2022 Hila Limar

Fawzia Koofi, pages 119–125 © 2022 Fawzia Koofi

Hosna Jalil, pages 127–134 © 2022 Hosna Jalil

Mina Sharif, pages 135, 137–147 © 2022 Mina Sharif

Rada Akbar, pages 149–166 © 2022 Rada Akbar

Conclusion, pages 167–170 © 2022 Nahid Shahalimi

Afterword, page 171 © 2022 Nahid Shahalimi

NAHID SHAHALIMI was born in Afghanistan and moved to Canada with her family when she was young. Today she lives in Germany where she works as an author, artist, and social entrepreneur. In 2017 she published her first book in German, *Where Courage Bears the Soul*, to great acclaim. The following year she released her award-winning film *We the Women of Afghanistan: A Silent Revolution*. *We Are Still Here* is her first English language publication.